— 150 —
BARS
YOU NEED
TO VISIT BEFORE
— YOU DIE —

LANNOO

OVERVIEW

OVERVIEW

OVERVIEW

ASIA

OCEANIA

Introduction

by Jurgen Lijcops

Everybody who knows me also knows that my first passion is wine. Until two years ago, it was also the only thread running through my work. Then along came Bar Burbure, an Antwerp cocktail bar that wants to be different from all others, and things took a new turn.

Before then, few people knew about my second passion: anything related to spirits. Not just spirits themselves, but everything surrounding and springing from them. For instance, cocktails and the bars that make and serve them. Also, the unique settings that are often offered by these bars and that make you enjoy your drinks even more.

Stepping into a bar is always a unique experience. You often feel the vibe at once, one that says that everything is okay and it is going to be a magical evening. This vibe is created by the people who work there, who attract other people with that same vibe who, in turn, enhance the vibe of the place.

I am proud to have had the opportunity to write this guide. Each and every bar I selected has a story to tell, which is certainly not always about the drinks. Often this story is told by the owners and the staff, or by the location.

In this book, I am going to take you on a journey around the world. We will be travelling to the US and South America, Europe, the United Kingdom, North Africa, Asia, and all the way to Australia. Enjoy it.

And ... cheers!

— 01 —
THE ROOFTOP

MEXICO

Cabo San Lucas

The Cape Hotel, Calle 12 entre 5 Avenida y 10 S/N,
Centro, 77710 Playa del Carmen, Q.R.

HOTEL
BAR

◆ TO VISIT BEFORE YOU DIE BECAUSE

This place has a unique holiday atmosphere. Combine this with the atmosphere of a rooftop bar and what do you get? Fun time!

The Rooftop sits atop a fantastic hotel in Mexico and is a bar of many talents. You can relax on one of many lounge beds, swim up to the bar in the pool, and sip fresh, refreshing drinks.

The gigantic terrace – almost 3,000 square metres – offers an incredible panoramic ocean view. In the evening it transforms into a popular open-air discotheque. Need we say more? This is about as close to paradise as you can get.

www.thompsonhotels.com/hotels/
cabo-san-lucas/the-cape-los-cabos/restaurant-bars/the-rooftop

— 02 —
THE AVIARY

UNITED
STATES

Chicago
955 West Fulton Market,
Chicago, IL 60607

COCKTAIL
BAR

◆ TO VISIT BEFORE YOU DIE BECAUSE

They serve three-, five- and seven-course cocktail- and
food-tasting menus that are to die for.

The Aviary is a three-star bar and treats its guests accordingly. No second-rate imitations here, but fabulous cocktails prepared in a state-of-the-art kitchen. The Aviary is universally acclaimed for its innovation and molecular preparations. Its famous 'Rooibos' cocktail is made by shaking rooibos tea with cinnamon, cardamom, saffron, vanilla, ground almonds, mint, verbena and lavender.

UNITED STATES	Chicago 111 West Kinzie Street, Chicago, IL 60654	COCKTAIL BAR

◆ TO VISIT BEFORE YOU DIE BECAUSE

The whisky list is super-impressive.

This bar looks a bit like a maze. Walk around and discover something new around every corner. The biggest space has live music and entertainment five nights a week. Next door you have a restaurant – five-times Michelin Bib Gourmand – headed by chef Ryan Pugh, a Champagne Room, Whiskey Room and several other bars. Untitled Supper Club boasts one of the largest selections of American whiskies and has special lockers for regular clients to store their bottles in. The menu lists about 15 knockout cocktails ranging from classics to contemporary mixes.

BORDEL

| UNITED STATES | Chicago
1721 West Division Street,
Chicago, IL 60622 | COCKTAIL BAR |

◆ TO VISIT BEFORE YOU DIE BECAUSE

In this place, you really, truly think you are the Great Gatsby.

Bordel is an experience in and of itself. As you might imagine, it conjures up images of a shady brothel, no doubt partly due to the red velvet and erotic posters lining the interior.

Have a classic cocktail while you enjoy the live flamenco performances. This sexy venue, with its equally sexy drinks, is the ideal place to get you in the mood. Order a 'Cherry Boom Boom' with bourbon, apple brandy, cinnamon and sour cherry, and let yourself be seduced.

— 05 —
EL FLORIDITA

	Havana	
CUBA	Obispo No.557 esq. a Monserrate Habana ViejaHavana	COCKTAIL BAR

◆ TO VISIT BEFORE YOU DIE BECAUSE

When you have a daiquiri here, you are not just drinking a good cocktail; you are drinking pure nostalgia!

This legendary bar (more than 200 years old), located in the older part of Havana, lies at the end of Obispo Street, across Monserrate Street, known for the National Museum of Fine Arts of Havana. El Floridita is said to be the birthplace of the daiquiri and was a regular haunt of Ernest Hemingway. He would drink his mojitos in La Bodeguita and his daiquiris in El Floridita. As Hemingway had diabetes, he would ask for sugar-free daiquiris. The recipe was named after him and is still popular among visitors. If you are going to have just one drink, make it a daiquiri. As for the bar's interior, the long counter is without doubt its most striking feature. Take a seat and let Cuban hospitality surprise you. The bar has a nice atmosphere but its patrons are almost exclusively tourists. Who knows, you might come across Naomi Campbell, Matt Dillon or Paco Rabanne. Besides cocktails, the bar also serves (rather pricy) fish dishes.

— 06 —
SLOPPY JOE'S BAR

Havana

Calle Zulueta 252 /
E Animas y Virtudes, Havana, 10100

COCKTAIL
BAR

◆ TO VISIT BEFORE YOU DIE BECAUSE

The 'Sloppy Joe' cocktail – brandy, port and Cointreau with a delicious touch of pineapple – is a cocktail to die for.

This bar, founded in 1917 by Spaniard José Abeal, was a hotspot for American tourists for decades. Its avant-garde clientele, long bar and illustrious patrons such as Ernest Hemingway and Spencer Tracy rightly earned it a reputation as one of the most legendary bars of the twentieth century. During the Prohibition era, celebrities flooded the bar as enthusiastically as alcohol flowed out of its taps and bottles. However, Sloppy Joe's was closed down in 1965. Over time the building became more and more dilapidated, but after almost half a century in ruins, it has now been restored to its former glory in an extensive refurbishment undertaken by the office of the Historian of Havana, headed by Eusebio Leal. Period photographs and accounts were used to restore the bar as faithfully as possible. The spectacular, 18-metre-long mahogany bar top proved to be the greatest challenge. Sloppy Joe's unique windows, too, were painstakingly restored. Thanks to these efforts, since 2013 Sloppy Joe's has become one of the most renowned venues in the cocktail business once again.

— 07 —
THE CHANDELIER LOUNGE

Las Vegas

The Cosmopolitan Hotel, 3708 South Las Vegas
Boulevard, Las Vegas, NV 89109

◆ TO VISIT BEFORE YOU DIE BECAUSE

The combination of the bar's unique interior and
perfect cocktails is not to be missed.

The Chandelier Lounge, just like the
general ambience in Las Vegas, is larger
than life. The bar sits in the centre of the
casino, right underneath a giant chandelier
composed of two million crystal beads. In
fact, the bar itself looks like a chandelier.
All of this creates an atmosphere you will
remember forever – if you do not drink
too many cocktails, of course. Drinks are
served on one of the bar's three floors,
which each have their own, characteristic
menu. The signature cocktails include
the 'Whiskey Business' – a new twist on
the classic 'Old-Fashioned' that mixes
Knob Creek bourbon with bitters, Amaro
Meletti and a home-made syrup – and the
'Finishing School', which pays tribute to
Alice in Wonderland with Ciroc Red Berry
vodka, strawberry-rhubarb syrup, citrus,
ginger beer and plum bitters.

— 08 —
GALLERY BAR

UNITED STATES	**Los Angeles** Biltmore Hotel, 506 Grand Avenue, Los Angeles, CA 90071	HOTEL BAR

◆ TO VISIT BEFORE YOU DIE BECAUSE

This bar lives within the legendary Biltmore Hotel, designed by Schultze & Weaver, probably two of the twentieth century's most important hotel architects.

An elegant hotel bar cum cognac room, the Gallery Bar's grandeur, with its chandeliers, leather banquettes and wooden furnishing, is reminiscent of an old library. The granite bar is the perfect place to sip an old-school Martini. This venue sits within the legendary Biltmore Hotel, designed by Schultze & Weaver, probably two of the twentieth century's most renowned hotel architects and the designers of, among others, the Waldorf Astoria in New York. The Gallery Bar is an ode to the end of the Prohibition era and the return of publicly served cocktails and other alcoholic drinks. Do try its signature 'Biltmore 1923' with its Botanist gin, Cointreau, Lillet Blanc and absinthe.

GIANNI BAR

UNITED
STATES

Los Angeles

The Nomad Los Angeles Hotel,
649 S Olive Street, Los Angeles, CA 90014

HOTEL
BAR

◆ TO VISIT BEFORE YOU DIE BECAUSE

This lobby bar is the kind of place you take a date to when you really want to impress them.

The Gianni Bar opened at the beginning of 2018. It is located inside the NoMad Los Angeles Hotel, which was once the head office of the Bank of Italy. In fact, the bar is named after Amadeo Gianni, the bank's founder.

Head bartender Leo Robitschek has composed a bar menu containing a wide range of cocktails, from all-time classics to fancy modern versions. This stylish lobby bar will really impress your date.

	Los Angeles	
UNITED STATES	7000 Hollywood Boulevard, Los Angeles, CA 90028	HOTEL BAR

◆ TO VISIT BEFORE YOU DIE BECAUSE

Where else can you throw some balls and sip a delicious coconut-infused vodka at the same time?

A bowling alley and hip cocktail lounge all in one? Only in Hollywood ... Brad Pitt and Alexander Skarsgard have been seen bowling at the Spare Room, and it's for a reason. The place has the finest bowling lanes you've ever seen – they are said to date back to the 1800s – and bowling shoes by George Esquivel. Not that everything in the Spare Room is about knocking down pins. To the contrary. The bowling alley is really more like a decor, an excuse for you to end up where you are supposed to end up: the bar. The bar rose to fame with founding father Aidan Demarest's world-renowned punch bowls, and now it has rising star Yael Vengroff shaking things up at the bar. The 27-year-old woman is worthy of our admiration not only for making Beverage Director at one of the world's best cocktail bars, but even more so for the twenty-something playfully surprising cocktails she mixes, including the stunning 'Bikini Kill' and its coconut-oil-infused vodka, passion fruit, Campari, Velvet Falernum, honey, and lime. As for recreational activities, bowling is but one of the various games they have lined up for you here. Is playing Monopoly or Scrabble from one of the Spare Room's velvet lounge chairs hip enough for you or what?

INNINGS
NAME 1 2 3 4 5 6 7 8 9 10 TALLY

BOUT
IQUE
LONDON

The
Cocktail
Party

The Spare Room

— 11 —
BLACKWELL RUM BAR

Negril

JAMAICA

The Caves Hotel, Lighthouse Road,
West End, Negril

HOTEL
BAR

◆ TO VISIT BEFORE YOU DIE BECAUSE

Here you can breathe Jamaica, and you taste it, too, because Jamaican rum will always be a little bit better than all the others.

This hotel bar is a pleasure to the eye. It is literally located inside the volcanic rocks of Negril's picturesque West End. The ocean view is complimentary. The Blackwell Rum Bar is a dramatic, beguiling space equipped with tables, benches and stools made of pieces of rock hewn out of the cliffs by local stonemasons.

Needless to say, if nothing else, what you order here is a drink made with Blackwell Rum, the brand of music producer Chris Blackwell, who breathed new life into his grandfather's recipe. Order it pure or go for the simple 'Goldeneye', which mixes it with fresh orange juice, pineapple juice and ground ice.

www.thecaveshotel.com/eat/blackwell-rum-bar/

— 12 —
BEACHBUM BERRY'S

UNITED
STATES

New Orleans
321 North Peters Street, New Orleans,
LA 70130

TIKI BAR

◆ TO VISIT BEFORE YOU DIE BECAUSE
Its cocktail menu covers the entire history of tiki drinking.

Back in the mid-1990s, when tiki cocktails had been a distant memory for years, one man succeeded in putting them back in the spotlight. That man was Jeff 'Beachbum' Berry, and with his book *Grog Log* he brought long-lost tiki recipes back to life. Since then, Jeff has published many more books and become a living legend, probably the world's most acclaimed tiki connoisseur. Hence the full name of this bar, Beachbum Berry's Latitude 29. This full-service restaurant and bar is an ode to the tiki: the exotic and lavishly adorned rum-based cocktail. It opened its doors in New Orleans's French Quarter in 2014 and almost immediately shot to the top. Its cocktail menu covers the entire history of tiki drinking, including the vintage recipes Jeff discovered and his own original recipes.

www.beachbumberry.com

— 13 —
CAROUSEL BAR

UNITED
STATES

New Orleans
214 Royal Street, New Orleans, LA 70130

COCKTAIL
BAR

◆ TO VISIT BEFORE YOU DIE BECAUSE
You need to have drunk their signature cocktail, the 'Vieux Carré',
at least once in your life.

This classic piano bar literally revolves like a carousel, so if you take a seat at the bar, you will also 'take a turn' before you are served your first drink. Having a hard time choosing? Try the 'Vieux Carré', the Carousel Bar's signature cocktail created by Walter Bergeron in 1938.

It is a blend of Bulleit Rye whiskey, Pierre Ferrand 1840, sweet vermouth, Bénédictine liqueur, and Angostura and Peychaud's bitters. The bar's decor is retro-like, and its patrons are a mix of tourists and locals.

UNITED STATES	New York 2nd floor, Pier A Harbor House, 22 Battery Place, New York, NY 10004	COCKTAIL BAR

◆ TO VISIT BEFORE YOU DIE BECAUSE

This bar specialises in cocktails from the Prohibition era.

The BlackTail Bar, located in Lower Manhattan in Battery Park, is a Cuban cocktail bar with a difference: that is, it does not just serve mojitos and cuba libres. While these are great drinks, the BlackTail Bar specialises in cocktails from the Prohibition era. Back in those days many Americans would take a quick flight to Havana to quench their thirst for alcohol. The planes flying them back and forth were called 'black tails'. The influx of weekend revellers caused an increase in the number of bars in Havana as well as new cocktail recipes for the Americans. The team behind BlackTail claims to have brought those Prohibition-era Cuban drinks to New York. The bar is reminiscent of Floridita, the birthplace of the daiquiri, on Havana's Obispo Street. The menu is divided into 'Highballs', 'Punches', 'Sours', 'Old-Fashioned', and 'Cocktails'. If you want to play it safe, then go for one of the well-known, classic Cuban cocktails, because they are fantastic. However, we also recommend something more adventurous, such as a 'Yankee Dollar' (bourbon, peated Scotch, peach, barley syrup, lime and soda) or a 'Gulf Stream' (mezcal, Irish whiskey, rum, falernum syrup, apple, dill, lime and maraschino).

— 15 —
THE BAR ROOM

UNITED STATES	New York The Beekman Hotel, 5 Beekman Street, New York, NY 10038	HOTEL BAR

◆ TO VISIT BEFORE YOU DIE BECAUSE

This establishment knows what really matters: delicious drinks, great food, lavish hospitality and cosy, stylish surroundings.

The Bar Room lies within the Beekman hotel and offers a unique setting where you can enjoy excellent cocktails and other drinks all through the day. The bar is part of the Temple Court restaurant, run by Tom Colicchio, and is located beneath a nine-storey Victorian atrium.

The numerous book cabinets and ubiquitous leather club chairs lend the bar a classy atmosphere that is enhanced by the portraits of famous authors – part of an extensive art collection – lining the walls.

— 16 —
THE BLOND

UNITED STATES	New York 11 Howard Street, New York, NY 10013	COCKTAIL BAR

◆ TO VISIT BEFORE YOU DIE BECAUSE

The atmosphere afterwork here is unique.
Dress to impress!

Start the evening in the Blond before moving on and livening up the streets of New York. It is especially known as an after-work watering hole and is one of the city's newer establishments. This is the kind of place you come to in order to show off. In other words: dress to impress.

— 17 —
CAMPBELL BAR

UNITED
STATES

New York
15 Vanderbilt Avenue, New York, NY 10017

COCKTAIL
BAR

◆ TO VISIT BEFORE YOU DIE BECAUSE

Try the 'Blonde Negroni' with Hendrick's Gin, Cocchi Americano and Suze.

The Gerber Group breathed new life into the Campbell Bar in New York's Grand Central Terminal. The bar opened its doors again in July 2016, retaining all of its former grandeur. Here you can enjoy a cosy lunch, savour various tapas and cold meat, and, of course, sip trendy drinks. The bar is divided into three spaces: the Campbell Bar, the Campbell Palm Court (an interior oasis and lounge encircled by towering palm trees) and the Campbell Terrace (a big covered veranda with a complete bar). Try the 'Blonde Negroni' with Hendrick's Gin, Cocchi Americano and Suze.

www.thecampbellnyc.com

— 18 —
DANTE

UNITED
STATES

New York

79–81 MacDougal Street, New York,
NY 10012

COCKTAIL
BAR

◆ TO VISIT BEFORE YOU DIE BECAUSE

You feel right away that this is a great place to be, especially when
the weather is fine and you can sit on the small terrace, enjoying
some bruschetta and sipping a negroni.

Dante is an iconic bar. It opened its
doors in 1915 and has been a favourite
with celebrities and artistic souls ever
since. The walls are lined with pictures
of Patti Smith, Ernest Hemingway,
Robert Mapplethorpe, Bob Dylan and Al
Pacino, all of whom have at some point
consumed cocktails at Dante. While this
world-famous establishment has received
a makeover, the past has been preserved
with respect. Dante is especially known
for its negroni and the many variations
on this classic drink's original recipe.
In fact, the original negroni with gin,
vermouth and Campari is dispensed on
tap, as is vermouth. The menu is also
graced with seasonal cocktails made with
fresh fruit, juices, vegetables and herbs.
But the evening starter or night closer for
many fans is the temptingly simple and
lovingly presented 'Garibaldi', with its
fresh orange juice and Campari.

www.dante-nyc.com

THE DEAD RABBIT

UNITED STATES	New York 30 Water Street, New York, NY 10004	COCKTAIL BAR

◆ TO VISIT BEFORE YOU DIE BECAUSE

What Petrus is to wine lovers, the Death Rabbit is to bar fans. Creations and ideas are hatched here that have a profound influence on the whole international bar scene.

This cocktail bar is a veritable icon, having won almost every prize there is to be won. In 2016 it was crowned best bar in the world, among other distinctions. The Dead Rabbit is inspired by old New York and Irish traditions, so no one will be surprised to learn that its two owners, Jack McGarry and Sean Muldoon, are from Ireland. Both men, possessed with the idea of making the perfect cocktail, managed to turn their American dream into reality. However, as they themselves are wont to say, they did not rush into their cocktail adventure. It took them six years to open

their bar. Today everybody knows them and where to find them, tucked away between the skyscrapers of New York's financial district. The Dead Rabbit comprises three floors. Downstairs is the 'Taproom', a cosy Irish pub serving mainly draught beer and whisky. The next floor is reserved for cocktails: classics, crazy versions of classics and contemporary delights. To give you an idea, the menu starts with a 'Sherry Cobbler' and finishes with a 'Hot Applejack Toddy'. The top floor is home to 'The Occasional', a private space by reservation only.

— 20 —
EMPLOYEES ONLY

UNITED
STATES

New York
510 Hudson Street, New York, NY 10014

COCKTAIL
BAR

◆ TO VISIT BEFORE YOU DIE BECAUSE

The bar undergoes a transformation when the sun goes down.
The ambience and vibe are simply unique.

In 2004 Dushan, Henry, Igor, Jay and Billy had a common goal: to open a local bar that would honour the craft of cocktail preparation. The result of their hard work and creativity is Employees Only, a grandiose bar with superb cocktails. It is also known for the thorough training it provides to its employees, ensuring that your cocktails are shaken and stirred by real pros. From its opening to today, Employees Only has offered a groundbreaking drinks menu whose best-known cocktails include the signature 'Manhattan' (to which they add Grand Marnier), the seasonal 'Ginger Smash' and the 'Amelia'. In the kitchen, chef Julia Jaksic takes a no-nonsense European-American approach to her dishes. Employees Only is a real success story, as evidenced by its expansion to Singapore, Panama City, Hong Kong and Miami. In their own words, they want to conquer the whole world …

Closed

— 21 —
NOMAD BAR

UNITED
STATES

New York
The Nomad Hotel, 10 West 28th Street,
New York, NY 10001

HOTEL
BAR

◆ TO VISIT BEFORE YOU DIE BECAUSE
The pub food here is traditional yet slightly different.

The NoMad Bar has it all: cocktails, fun music, trendy parties and seriously good food. Bar manager Leo Robitschek manages to surprise guests with pub food that is traditional yet slightly different. He is also inventive with his cocktails. Think rare spirits and surprising techniques.

The bar has a warm, welcoming interior, including the library and lounge. And did you know that cocktail legend Jerry Thomas opened his first bar in this very street? NoMad is currently planning to open a second bar in Los Angeles.

— 22 —
ATTABOY

UNITED
STATES

New York
134 Eldridge Street, New York, NY 10002

COCKTAIL
BAR

◆ TO VISIT BEFORE YOU DIE BECAUSE
They serve a wonderfully refreshing evergreen cocktail, which you should try not to miss: the 'Gold Rush', made with whisky and honey.

There are few hidden bars or speakeasies to be found in New York these days, but Attaboy is one. Standing in front of the ugly, brown entrance, you would never know that cocktail heaven is waiting for you right behind it. Here they make cocktails to order, so there is no menu, just drinks concocted to your taste. Tell the bartender what you like and they will fix you something unique. At the bar watch owners Sam Ross and Michael McIlroy ply their trade from up close and prepare to be impressed. The decor and atmosphere are typically speakeasy: 1920s and not too brightly lit. Nice to know: this space used to house Milk & Honey, Sasha Petraske's iconic cocktail bar.

MACE

UNITED STATES	New York	COCKTAIL BAR
	649 East 9th Street, New York, NY 10009	

◆ TO VISIT BEFORE YOU DIE BECAUSE

Try the signature cocktail 'Mace', with Aperol, aquavit, beet juice, orange acid, young Thai coconut cordial and mace mist.

Mace is located in New York's East Village where botanicals take centre stage. It was created by Greg Boehm and Nicolas de Soto and serves drinks inspired by flavours and aromas from the world of herbs. While its cocktail menu is not extensive, all the drinks are revelations. How about the signature cocktail 'Mace', with Aperol, aquavit, beet juice, orange acid, young Thai coconut cordial and mace mist? The bar is named after the spice mace, which is the dried aril or seed coat of nutmeg. If you feel adventurous, ask for the 'Damiana', a cocktail with shiitake-infused pisco, banana liqueur, lemon juice, bitters, oat albumin, pandan (rice) syrup and Damiana bitters. Behind the bar are racks of herbs and all kinds of mysteries preserved in jars.

www.macenewyork.com

MONARCH ROOFTOP

UNITED STATES	New York	HOTEL BAR
	Courtyard Marriott Manhattan, 71 West 35th Street, New York, NY 10018	

◆ TO VISIT BEFORE YOU DIE BECAUSE

The view from this place is one of a kind.

Monarch Rooftop is the newest undertaking by Ric Addison and Stephen Daly, the team behind the Ava Rooftop Lounge. Located on the 18th floor of the Courtyard Marriott Manhattan, this bar has a stunning view of the Empire State Building. The stylish interior is very open, with lots of light and Scandinavian influences. On the terrace you can indulge in impressive sunsets over New York, the city that never sleeps. The house specialities are the small-batch gins and the cinnamon-infused home-made bourbon. If you like a serious kick, order the 'Butterfly Effect' with its tequila and jalapeños. This hotel bar also serves delicious small bites and some really cool desserts.

MR PURPLE

New York
Hotel Indigo, 180 Orchard Street,
New York, NY 10002

◆ TO VISIT BEFORE YOU DIE BECAUSE

This wonderful combination of roof bar and hotel bar has a very special personality of its own.

Mr Purple is located on the 15th floor of Hotel Indigo, Lower East Side, and is the brainchild of internationally renowned design bureau Crème Design. Its interior occupies a whopping 3,000 square metres and it has two exterior terraces overlooking New York.

The big terrace on the west side even has a swimming pool and a bar of its own. You will certainly not want for choice where drinks are concerned, either. Order their modern versions of the 'GG Manhattan' or the 'Old-Fashioned' and prepare for a surprise.

www.mrpurplenyc.com

UNITED STATES	**San Francisco** 3010 20th Street, San Francisco, CA 94110	**COCKTAIL BAR**

◆ TO VISIT BEFORE YOU DIE BECAUSE

The drinks are perfectly balanced and – very importantly – have little or no garnish.

Trick Dog is the creation of Josh Harris, Scott Baird and Jason Henton, aka 'The Bon Vivants', who had the ingenious idea of taking an old factory building and turning it into a trendy bar, one where you look around and what you see says 'industrial', but what you hear is Motown, funk and soul. Not surprisingly, the bar has carried off numerous awards. Twice a year head bartender Kim Roselle and her team come up with a skill second to none, and twice a year she and her team come up with a completely new menu. The 11th edition (beginning of 2018), christened 'Trick Dog Airways', comes in the form of a safety card like the ones you find in all commercial aircraft, and its cocktails are named after important international airport terminals. Take the 'CDG', after Charles De Gaulle airport in Paris, which features Michter's rye, Cynar, Noilly Prat and 'waffle liqueur'.

— 27 —
RED2ONE

Santiago

CHILE

W Santiago Hotel, Isidora Goyenechea 3000 – Las Condes,
Santiago, Región Metropolitana

HOTEL
BAR

◆ TO VISIT BEFORE YOU DIE BECAUSE

This bar tells the story of a unique region and its products:
la Región Metropolitana de Chile.

Elegant and sophisticated would be a good way to describe the RED2ONE bar, which is located on the rooftop of the W Santiago hotel. Its cocktails are inspired by Chile's four geographical areas: north (intense and spirited), south (fruity and aromatic), east (sweet and warm) and west (sour and fizzy).

Our favourites? The 'Peanuts & Honey' from the north, with its peanut-infused bourbon, honey syrup and Angostura bitters, and also the 'Chilenita' from the west, which mixes pisco, falernum syrup, lime, cucumber and mint. However, do travel to the south and east, too …

— 28 —
CANON BAR

UNITED
STATES

Seattle
928 12th Avenue, Seattle, WA 98122

COCKTAIL
BAR

◆ TO VISIT BEFORE YOU DIE BECAUSE

Nothing is too outlandish or far-fetched at the Canon Bar. Have you ever had a drink served to you in a plasma bag? Ask for a 'Transfusion 4'.

In the Canon Bar you have choice aplenty, for it boasts over 4,000 different brands of spirit. No wonder the bar looks like a library, with bookshelves chock-full of bottles and even a ladder to reach the top shelves. The Canon Bar is all about whisky and bitters, so much so that they literally ingrained the bar's wood with Angostura bitters, giving it its rich, brown colour. The owner has done everything possible to satisfy everybody's preferences and tastes: from simple three-piece cocktails to spectacular shows of smoke and fire.

www.canonseattle.com

— 29 —
RUMBA

UNITED
STATES

Seattle
1112 Pike Street,
Seattle, WA 98101

TIKI BAR

◆ TO VISIT BEFORE YOU DIE BECAUSE
Their empanadas are super-tasty.

Rumba will blow you away with its
enormous range of rums: there are more
than 200 of them! The exotic cocktails
in this classic tiki bar will have you
daydreaming of tropical beaches. The bar,
with an atmosphere as lively as its decor,
also serves attractive dishes based on
Caribbean cuisine.

CANADA

Toronto
505 College Street,
Toronto, ON M6G 1A4

COCKTAIL
BAR

◆ TO VISIT BEFORE YOU DIE BECAUSE

When you enter this bar, you step into the world of Antoni Gaudí.

El Raval, a neighbourhood in Barcelona that is renowned for its nightlife and cabaret, is a cultural melting pot with a vibrant atmosphere, just like Bar Raval in Toronto. Enter here and you will feel like you have been transported to a typical Spanish tapas bar, with various small dishes lining the counter. The tapas are best accompanied with the perfectly paired vermouth-and sherry-based drinks that make up most of the well-thought-out drinks list. You also have the unusual option of choosing 'low-octane' cocktails; that is, cocktails low in alcohol. Alternatively, may we suggest the surprising 'Canyonero' agave cocktail with its Siete Misterios Doba-Yej mezcal, Los Altos Plata Blanco, RinQuinQuin à la Pêche, lime, agave and Angostura bitters.

Vermouth Rosé

Fill a tumbler glass with ice
cubes and the following:
60 ml (1/4 cup) of Vermouth Belsazar Rosé
Garnish with orange or blood-orange zest.

Corpse Reviver

Chill a coupette glass. Add a bar spoon of
absinthe and swirl it around to coat the glass.

Fill a shaker with ice cubes and the following:
→ 25 ml (5 teaspoons) Ferdinand's Saar Quince
→ 20 ml (4 teaspoons) Triple Sec
→ 20 ml (4 teaspoons) Forest Vermouth White
→ 20 ml (4 teaspoons) lime juice

Shake for 20 seconds and strain into the chilled
glass. Garnish with lime zest.

Mocktail Erasmus Bond Botanical

Take a chilled coupette glass.
Add an ice cube or ice ball.
Serve the cool Erasmus Bond
Botanical tonic water with care and
garnish with a sprig of thyme.

Moscow Mule

Take a long-drink glass and fill
with the following:
→ 50 ml (1/5 cup) Grey Goose vodka
→ 120 ml (1/2 cup) Erasmus Bond Dry Ginger
→ Ice cubes
→ Juice of half a lime
→ 2 ml (3/8 teaspoon) Angostura bitters

Normandy Eggnog

Chill a wine glass. Pour a dash (0.625 ml or
1/8 teaspoon) of egg white into a shaker,
briefly shake very hard and then fill the
shaker with ice cubes and the following:
→ 30 ml (2 tablespoons) Calvados Drouin
→ 20 ml (4 teaspoons) Drouin apple cider
→ 10 ml (2 teaspoons) Poire William
→ 15 ml (1 tablespoon) milk
→ 15 ml (1 tablespoon) Chardonnay cordial
→ 15 ml (1 tablespoon) cream
→ 1 complete egg

Shake everything hard and
serve in the chilled glass.

Cocktail
intermezzo

Porto Cooler

Fill a long-drink glass with ice
cubes and the following:
→ 50 ml (1/5 cup) Porto White Graham's
→ 10 ml (2 teaspoons) lime juice
→ 150 ml (3/5 cup) Erasmus Bond Tonic Dry

— 31 —
FLYING DUTCHMEN COCKTAILS

THE NETHERLANDS	Amsterdam Singel 460, 1017 AW, Amsterdam	COCKTAIL BAR

◆ TO VISIT BEFORE YOU DIE BECAUSE

Bartenders Tess and Timo are at the top of their field and mix classic cocktails the traditional way or with a twist.

This cocktail bar opened in the historic Odeon building in Amsterdam at the end of 2017. The creators of this new hotspot in the Dutch capital are Tess Posthumus and Timo Janse, who are certainly no strangers on the Amsterdam cocktail scene. Tess was elected best Dutch bartender at the 2015 Diageo World Class competition. She went on to win the title of Best Female Bartender Worldwide at the world finals in Cape Town. Her business partner Timo has won many national and international cocktail awards in recent years, in addition to writing the non-alcoholic-cocktail book *Shake It*. Both have a ten-year career at speakeasy bar Doors 47 behind them. Now, in their new cocktail bar, they are focusing on mixing classic cocktails the traditional way or with a special twist of their own. They also organise workshops and courses on the stories behind the classic drinks, their recipes and the history of the bartenders who created them.

THE NETHERLANDS	Amsterdam Lijnbaanssteeg 5–7, 1012 TE, Amsterdam	COCKTAIL BAR

◆ TO VISIT BEFORE YOU DIE BECAUSE

The 'Old-Fashioned' cocktails they serve here are truly exceptional.

Tales & Spirits is rather the odd one out here. It looks more like a village pub than a trendy place to be. But then again, maybe that is exactly what makes it hip ... Since its opening in the centre of Amsterdam in 2012, the bar has put its mark on the Dutch cocktail scene.

Owners Lydia Soedadi and Boudewijn Mesritz managed to get Tales & Spirits on the 'World's 50 Best Bars' list in just two years. The drinks they serve are exquisite, and they are famous for their home-made shrubor vinegar-based syrups. All cocktails on the menu have a story to tell, and the 'Old-Fashioned' section is exceptional. On top of all this, you can treat yourself to a magnificent dinner here.

BELGIUM

Antwerp
Graaf van Egmontstraat 20,
2000 Antwerp

COCKTAIL
BAR

◆ TO VISIT BEFORE YOU DIE BECAUSE

They serve delicious home-made spirits and pre-batch cocktails.

Ben Belmans and Dieter Van Roy, two creative mixologists, opened BelRoy's Bijou in Antwerp's Zuid area in March 2016. The cocktail bar immediately shot to the top, winning the title of 'Best Cocktail Bar' at the 2016 Venuez Hospitality Awards less than a year after opening! With a team like the one at BelRoy's Bijou, this is not a surprise. Not only did Dries Botty win the 'Best Belgian Bartender' award in 2016, but he also ranked fourth in the 'World Class Bartender of the Year'. This cosy bar focuses on flavours and quality products. Its talented team mixes classic cocktails, of course, but it also makes its own creations and serves a fine selection of snacks. Fancy a real Bijou cocktail? Go for the 'Rose Garden', a classic Cosmopolitan with a creative Dieter Van Roy touch that combines home-made rosemary syrup, lemon and aquafaba (the liquid from canned chickpeas). In December 2017, under the name of 'BelRoy's, bartenders & distillers', the bar's founders, Ben and Dieter, launched six liquors of their own: a gin, a vodka, a rum and three bottle-aged cocktails – 'Vesper Martini', 'Negroni' and 'El Presidente'. This is a great place in Antwerp's Zuid for an appetiser or after-dinner drinks.

— 34 —
DOGMA

BELGIUM

Antwerp
Wijngaardstraat 5,
2000 Antwerp

COCKTAIL
BAR

◆ TO VISIT BEFORE YOU DIE BECAUSE

The bartenders here proudly use only the highest-quality ingredients and provide service worthy of a Michelin-starred restaurant.

Dogma is one of Antwerp's best-known cocktail bars. With a decor consisting of vintage leather seats and an equally eye-catching bar counter, it has a mainly retro look with a heavy dose of rock 'n' roll. Owner and mixologist Didier Van den Broeck is well known both in Belgium and abroad. He won third place in the 2014 Diageo World Class Belgium competition and the 'Best Bartender' award at the 2016 Venuez Hospitality Awards. At the end of 2017 he made it to the Bacardi Legacy Competition world finals in Mexico, which has the world's best bartenders competing against each other with cocktails of their own creation. Van den Broeck's abundant creativity and know-how leap from the menu with his own versions of classics and his daring signature cocktails, such as the 'Aix en Provence' with its apple brandy, honey, thyme, orange, lemon, IPA and goats-cheese foam. Dogma has, without a doubt, put its mark on the Belgian cocktail scene since 2013, proudly using only the highest-quality ingredients and providing service worthy of a Michelin-starred restaurant.

www.dogmacocktails.be

ALEXANDER'S BAR

GREECE

Athens
Hotel Grande Bretagne,
Constitution Square, Athens, 105 64

HOTEL
BAR

◆ TO VISIT BEFORE YOU DIE BECAUSE

Here you will find rare single-malt whiskies, brandies and cognacs.

Alexander's Bar in Athens is definitely one of the best hotel bars in the world. It boasts an inviting interior, warm atmosphere and top-quality drinks. Here you will find rare single- malt whiskies, brandies and cognacs. Just reading the drinks lists is guaranteed to make your mouth water. Fancy a cocktail instead? Then go for the bar's signature 'Mandarin Napoleon Select', a blend of Dubonnet Rouge, Grand Marnier, gin and fragrant essential oil of Sicilian tangerines. The origin of the venue's name becomes clear when you enter, because behind the bar hangs a rare eighteenth-century tapestry portraying Alexander the Great at the battle of Gaugamela.

— 36 —
THE CLUMSIES

GREECE

Athens
Praxitelous 30, Athens, 105 61

COCKTAIL
BAR

◆ TO VISIT BEFORE YOU DIE BECAUSE
This bar has a legendary private room (by reservation only) complete with
bookcase, pool table, old-school records and crackling fireplace.

The Clumsies is an 'all-day' bar, and the brilliant brainchild of two popular Greek bartenders: Vassilis Kyritsis and Nikos Bakoulis, who met in 2012 behind – what a coincidence – a bar counter. Things immediately clicked between them, and a few years later they opened their own bar together with three enterprising businessmen. The bar's interior is bathed in natural light, its pale wood and white and turquoise decor highlighting the airy feel that the bar wants to radiate during the day. As the day changes into evening, The Clumsies turns into a hip hotspot where unique cocktails take centre stage. The bar's name may have you thinking otherwise, but the experienced barmen know how to handle a shaker. Two cocktails that are certainly worthy of mention are the 'Chilli con Melon' and the 'Gizmo'. The former, with its premium tequila, mezcal, melon, sage and a chipotle, packs a superior punch, while the latter's bourbon, pink grapefruit, sherry and dried olive leaves provide a uniquely Greek experience. The jewel in the Clumsies' crown is its legendary private room (by reservation only), complete with bookcase, pool table, old-school records and crackling fireplace.

www.theclumsies.gr

— 37 —
APOTHEKE

SPAIN

Barcelona
Plaça Reial 13–15,
08002 Barcelona

COCKTAIL
BAR

◆ TO VISIT BEFORE YOU DIE BECAUSE
The whole place exudes mystery, and the drinks are great …

Located on Barcelona's Plaça Reial, Ocaña houses a restaurant, a nightclub and … Apotheke cocktail bar, a breathtaking place characterised by a passion for antiques and respect for craftsmanship. The result is a combination of various styles: old chandeliers, a wooden church floor, massive pillars and works by contemporary artists.

In Apotheke the drinks are the stars of the night, but they share the limelight with the able bartenders. Owner Mario Grünenfelde, one of Berlin's most famous barmen, loves to add oriental flavours to his cocktails. We suggest you ask for a 'Flesh & Blood', made with gin, Moroccan lavender syrup and kaffir lime leaves.

— 38 —
EL NACIONAL

SPAIN

Barcelona
Passeig de Gràcia 24 Bis,
08007 Barcelona

COCKTAIL
BAR

◆ TO VISIT BEFORE YOU DIE BECAUSE

This bar stands out because of its sheer size, but also because of its top quality and the very special experience it provides.

Since El Nacional opened its doors in 2014 it has enjoyed the distinction of being the largest restaurant in Barcelona. The complex covers a huge 2,600 square metres and contains no fewer than four different restaurants, four bars and four gastropubs. Before becoming El Nacional, the building was first a theatre and then a car park full of pop-up stores. In its new guise the place is a real hotspot. The entrance to El Nacional is at the end of an inconspicuous alley off the Passeig de Gràcia. Once inside, you come to a big room that has been divided into different spaces, each of which is a veritable paradise for food lovers. In the middle of it all sits El Nacional's cocktail bar. Serving vermouth with assorted snacks during the daytime, it switches to various bold signature cocktails in the evening.

DRY MARTINI BAR

Barcelona

SPAIN

Carrer d'Aribau 162–166,
08036 Barcelona

COCKTAIL
BAR

◆ TO VISIT BEFORE YOU DIE BECAUSE
You can take a Dry Martini seminar from master Pedro Carbonell himself.

In a bar that goes by the name of the Dry Martini Bar, what else can you have but dry Martinis? Of course, they know how to make them to perfection. Pedro Carbonell, the founder of the bar, stirred his first dry Martini here in 1978. The ambience is classy and 007 would wear this bar like a second skin. Situated in Barcelona's Eixample neighbourhood, the Dry Martini Bar mainly draws crowds looking for the best cocktails. The discreet bartenders, trained at the nearby Martini Academy, ensure that the drinks are top-quality at all times. The fact that more than one million Martinis have been served here can only mean one thing: they know how to make a proper one! There is no way you will walk out of this venue feeling anything but satisfied.

www.drymartiniorg.com

— 40 —
EDGBASTON BAR

UNITED
KINGDOM

Birmingham
The Edgbaston, 18 Highfield Road,
Birmingham, B15 3DU

HOTEL BAR

◆ TO VISIT BEFORE YOU DIE BECAUSE
This bar has succeeded in recreating the grandeur of yore.

The Edgbaston is a Victorian-inspired bar run by brothers Darren and Stuart Insall in a stylish boutique hotel less than two kilometres from the centre of Birmingham. There is a lot of attention to detail, and much effort has been put into re-creating the grandeur of yore. The Edgbaston Bar is actually three bars. Each has its own individual ambience while still retaining uniformity with the others. Head bartender Rob Wood's cocktail menu, inspired by Japan and the James Bond girls, boasts no fewer than 87 drinks divided into four themes: sweet, dry, refreshing and boozy. Delectable mocktails also feature prominently and the home-made lemonade is delicious too.

www.theedgbaston.co.uk

HUMUS x HORTENSE

BELGIUM	**Brussels** Rue de Vergnies 2, 1050 Brussels	COCKTAIL BAR

◆ TO VISIT BEFORE YOU DIE BECAUSE

They combine excellent cocktails with vegetable dishes whose ingredients come straight from local producers.

Humus x Hortense is the brainchild of three creative minds. Chef Nicolas Decloedt, mixologist Matthieu Chaumont, and ceramist/sommelière Caroline Baerten joined together to make this surprising concept a reality. They serve both excellent cocktails and vegetable dishes prepared with ingredients coming straight from local producers.

Humus x Hortense is a cool cross-over in an interior reminiscent of an English tea salon. In the evening, however, when the lights are dimmed, you immediately feel as if you are in a clubby cocktail bar. The fantastic wines are certainly worth trying, too. Of course, as befits the concept, they are all organic.

SEIBERTS BAR

GERMANY

Cologne
Friesenwall 33, 50672 Cologne, Germany

COCKTAIL BAR

The liquid chef uses the most advanced techniques and equipment for his presentations and mixes.

The exceptional atmosphere in Volker Seibert's bar in Cologne is more like that of a majestic hotel than of a place where drinks are served. Volker Seibert is one of the world's best mixologists. He ran Cologne's Capri Lounge for 15 years until he opened his own bar in 2014. Visitors to Seibert's Classic Bar & Liquid Kitchen are spoiled by lots of attention to detail. The decor immediately reminds you of the 1920s. The big chandeliers, heavy curtains and Chesterfield sofas give the interior its particular look. The focal point is the custom-made bar counter that makes patrons want to hang around for far too long. The fantastic wine menu is worth mentioning, but what really makes Seiberts Bar so unique is the cocktails. No one combines old-school cocktails and new creations with the latest bar trends like Seibert. With his great experience of the tastes, aromas and possibilities of distilled beverages, he very aptly calls his bar a liquid kitchen. You can safely refer to it as food pairing with cocktails, a craft that Seibert masters down to the last detail. There is even a Volker's Tea Time, a cocktail workshop taught by the master himself. If you want to enrol, be quick about it, though, because the workshops are fully booked months in advance.

PRINCE OF
WALES BAR

Cong

IRELAND

Ashford Castle, Leaf Island, Cong,
Co. Mayo, F31 CA48

HOTEL
BAR

◆ TO VISIT BEFORE YOU DIE BECAUSE

This bar is located in the magnificent Ashford Castle in Ireland,
a place that exudes luxury.

The Prince of Wales Bar can be found in the magnificent Ashford Castle in Ireland. The castle exudes luxury and has been privileged to receive visits by such famous people as Oscar Wilde, John Lennon, Brad Pitt and the Princess of Monaco. Built in 1228, the castle was recently renovated. Film director John Ford shot most of his classic *The Quiet Man* (1952) in the grounds of Ashford Castle and in neighbouring Cong. The nineteenth-century bar is truly a magical place that will make you feel like you are in heaven. Although the cocktail menu looks classic, it fits perfectly with the spirit of the castle. It has a wide choice of drinks, and a notable selection of liqueurs and brandies.

www.ashfordcastle.com/food-and-drink/the-prince-of-wales-bar

— 44 —
BUZA BAR

CROATIA

Dubrovnik
Crijevićeva Ulica 9, 20000 Dubrovnik

COCKTAIL
BAR

◆ TO VISIT BEFORE YOU DIE BECAUSE

Not only can you enjoy a perfectly served cocktail here, but you are also treated to a breathtaking view of the Adriatic.

This bar is probably located at one of the most beautiful places in the world. Not only can you enjoy a perfectly served cocktail here, but you are also treated to a breathtaking view of the Adriatic. What more could you want?

The Buza Bar is also rather aptly called 'the hole in the wall': 'buza' means 'hole' in the Dubrovnik dialect, and to enter this magical place you indeed have to step through a hole in the wall. Note: the bar is open only during the spring and summer months.

— 45 —
THE COBBLER

BELGIUM

Ghent
Graslei 16, 9000 Ghent

HOTEL
BAR

◆ TO VISIT BEFORE YOU DIE BECAUSE

This is a marvellous bar located in a marvellous building along the marvellous canals of marvellous Ghent.

The Cobbler opened its doors in August 2017 in the former Hôtel des Postes et des Télégraphes, recently renamed the Zannier Hotel 1898 The Post. Located on the first floor of this historical post office building, the bar welcomes both hotel guests and non-guests. The bar is crewed by none other than Jurgen Nobels and David Lebeer, two giants of the cocktail world, who cater to their guests' every need. The Cobbler serves premium spirits, fresh juices and herbs, and unusual brews created by the bartenders themselves. The bar is named after the eponymous cocktail and shaker. And appropriately the house cocktails, or 'Cobblers', are served in the Cobbler shaker. The cocktail menu is divided into such sections as 'Aperitivos', 'Refreshing', 'Fruit & Tropical', 'Savoury & Experimental', 'Short & Strong', 'Dessert Cocktails', 'Hot Cocktails', etc. If alcohol is not your thing, there are also non-alcoholic versions in every section. Drinking is not all you can do at the Cobbler. You can also have breakfast (by reservation), enjoy a light lunch, eat a cake with a cup of coffee, or indulge in the original tapas and bar bites. The Cobbler's nineteenth-century artworks and antiques lend it an air of intrigue, with the high ceilings, open fireplace, and wooden floorboards giving the finishing touches. It is not a matter of elitism, but of creating a welcoming atmosphere that tempts you to linger just a little too long ...

www.zannierhotels.com/1898thepost/en/experience/the-cobbler/

— 46 —
JIGGER'S

BELGIUM

Ghent
Oudburg 16, 9000 Ghent

COCKTAIL
BAR

◆ TO VISIT BEFORE YOU DIE BECAUSE
Olivier Jacobs was the first Belgian bartender to attain international fame.

Owner Olivier Jacobs earned his stripes in Café Theatre near the courthouse in Ghent, opening his own speakeasy cocktail bar in 2012. Jigger's was an instant hit, repeatedly winning a place among the world's 100 best cocktail bars. Jacobs himself was crowned best Benelux bartender in the 2011 and 2012 editions of the Diageo World Class Bartender competition. Now, five years after its inauguration, he has expanded his bar. There is no doorbell any more, and patrons can enjoy the most surprising drinks in the basement bar, the new bar on the ground floor, and the front and back terraces. The bar's name, too, has been expanded, from Jiggers to Jigger's Coolers & Cocktails. 'Coolers' are for easy drinking, while 'Cocktails' refers to more refined, original flavours. Everything is made in-house, except the spirits themselves. The Jigger's Team continues to go out of its way to serve the perfect cocktail and create a worldly atmosphere, alongside its challenging and innovative menu.

HR GIGER BAR

SWITZER LAND

Gruyères
Rue du Château St Germain 3,
1630 Gruyères

COCKTAIL BAR

◆ TO VISIT BEFORE YOU DIE BECAUSE

You can daydream while you drink in the fairy tale-like decor.

The renowned Giger Bar is located in Château St Germain, the home of the Museum HR Giger, where Swiss artist H.R. Giger's surrealistic *oeuvre* is on display. You may not have heard Giger's name before, but you will certainly be familiar with the film *Alien* (1979). Giger's design for the film's monster earned him an Oscar in 1980. Since its inauguration in 1998, the Museum HR Giger has been the repository of the largest collection of works by Giger. The museum bar, too, is a must for all fans of the artist. Giger himself, who sadly passed away in 2014, designed the whole interior, including the bar counter and furniture. Come and enjoy a cocktail in this fantastical decor inside the belly of the beast ...

www.hrgiger.com/barmuseum

BOILERMAN BAR

GERMANY	**Hamburg**	COCKTAIL
	Osakaallee 12, 20457 Hamburg	BAR

◆ TO VISIT BEFORE YOU DIE BECAUSE

German *Gründlichkeit* rules this bar that specialises in Highballs, shots of spirits mixed with a carbonated beverage.

Owners Jörg Meyer and Rainer Wendt opened their first Boilerman Bar in Eppendorf and the second one in Hamburg. In the Boilerman Bars you drink 'Highballs' and that's it. No discussion. After all, the bar's slogan is 'We got balls'. Theoretically, a Highball is a shot of spirit mixed with a sizeable quantity of carbonated beverage. Drinks are not shaken here, just stirred. The Boilerman Bar specialises in rum Highballs, but it also makes Highballs with whisky, tequila and gin, all of them served in chilled glasses with two big ice cubes. The term 'Highball' refers to the white globes that were formerly used on American railways to signal to train drivers that they were running behind schedule and had to accelerate. The boilerman was the person firing the engine, hence the name of this popular bar. The Boilerman Bar is located in the 25hours Hotel Altes Hafenamt.

www.boilerman-hafenamt.de

LE LION BAR DE PARIS

GERMANY	**Hamburg** Rathausstraße 3, 20095 Hamburg	COCKTAIL BAR

◆ TO VISIT BEFORE YOU DIE BECAUSE

The high-level German hospitality at Le Lion Bar is exceptional.

Le Lion Bar, with its striking golden lion behind the counter, is probably one of the most conspicuous cocktail bars in Germany. It is headed by well-known, award-winning bartender Jörg Meyer, who also runs his own blog. The bar radiates a sophisticated yet unpretentious atmosphere, and the bartenders, true professionals with an almost encyclopedic knowledge of cocktails, serve drinks of unprecedented quality with the utmost care and love. Le Lion is not your cheapest bar, but the quality and experience you get here are worth every penny. Come and drink fantastic world-class cocktails, but do remember to book a table.

www.lelion.net

— 50 —
THE ALLIS

TURKEY

Istanbul
Soho House, Evliya Çelebi Mahallesi,
34430 Beyoğlu/Istanbul

**COCKTAIL
BAR**

◆ TO VISIT BEFORE YOU DIE BECAUSE

They offer not only tasty, classic cocktails, but also the opportunity for quiet,
relaxing moments in the interior garden and walks along the shoreline.

The Allis is a lounge bar named after
Charles Allis, an industrialist and renowned
art collector. During the day, the bar serves
light snacks; in the evening, Istanbul's night
owls descend on the place to savour its
sophisticated cocktails. You can also drop by
for an afternoon tea and enjoy the view of
the Palazzo Corpi.

— 51 —
KILIMANJARO

Istanbul

TURKEY

MerkezMah. Silahşör Cad. BirahaneSok. No: 1,
TarihiBomontiBiraFabrikası, 34384 Şişli/İstanbul

COCKTAIL
BAR

◆ TO VISIT BEFORE YOU DIE BECAUSE

You will rarely see such a thoroughly Turkish
and yet Scandinavian-looking decor.

Kilimanjaro is a recently inaugurated bar-restaurant located in the historic Bomonti beer brewery. Its name appeals to the imagination, and its jazzy interior overwhelms the senses with its solid-wood panelling, brick walls, huge windows and, in the middle of it all, a very peculiar bar.

The menu is inspired by, but not restricted to, Turkish cuisine. From its own fresh take on enginar salad with orange sauce to the lahanasarma (stuffed cabbage leaves) filled with broad beans, its dishes are fingerlickingly good. Kilimanjaro's cocktails are along the same lines: fresh and classic, but always inventive.

www.kilimanjaroist.com

— 52 —
GRA Z VOGNEM

UKRAINE

Kiev
Kreshhatik Street 6, Kiev

COCKTAIL
BAR

◆ TO VISIT BEFORE YOU DIE BECAUSE

You will stand a good chance of seeing local fashion models and celebrities in this hip bar.

This bar-restaurant devotes great attention to the local cuisine of Ukraine. Chef Alexander Yakutov is well known because he used to be a popular participant in a Ukrainian reality show. His dishes, too, are known far beyond Ukraine. He works in an open kitchen, approaching traditional cuisine from an innovative angle. His cocktail menu also pays tribute to Ukraine. Bartender Dmitro Dred elegantly demonstrates his skill by pairing his drinks perfectly with chef Alexander's recipes. Think local fruit, berries and premium spirits. Definitely worth a try.

— 53 —
STOLLEN 1930

AUSTRIA

Kufstein
Römerhofgasse 4, 6330 Kufstein

COCKTAIL BAR

◆ TO VISIT BEFORE YOU DIE BECAUSE

The bar has its own gin, the Stollen 1930, made with ginger and pepper.

Kufstein in Tirol may be one of Austria's smallest towns, but it is home to the world's biggest gin collection, Stollen 1930. The bar's collection of 800 different types of gin earned it an entry in the *Guinness Book of Records*. While gin lovers from all over the world flock to this trendy, speakeasy bar, staunch purists will also be satisfied. The music and ambience do Stollen 1930 full justice, too, because you immediately feel like you have stepped into a scene from *The Great Gatsby*. Since we are in ski country, this is a great place to unwind after skiing or snowboarding.

www.auracher-loechl.at/de/stollen-1930/102-0.html

— 54 —
RED FROG BAR

PORTUGAL

Lisbon
Rua do Salitre 5A, 1250–196 Lisbon

COCKTAIL
BAR

◆ TO VISIT BEFORE YOU DIE BECAUSE

This bar brings back to life the periods in history that stimulated the rise in popularity of spirits.

When you step beyond the big door with the red frog on one of Portugal's most expensive streets, you discover a mystical place that mixes magical cocktails. It is a place that also boasts an in-depth knowledge of the history of drinks. In fact, it claims to bring back to life the periods in history that stimulated the rise in popularity of spirits. Think of the beginning of the nineteenth century, or the revolutionary period from 1950 to 1970, or the resurgence of the cocktail in the 1990s. However, this attention to the past does not mean that today's cocktails and the combining of exceptional tastes and techniques are neglected. Red Frog Speakeasy is a classy bar that has a lot of respect for all that is poured into a glass. You have never seen cocktails finished the way they are here, and the bar's atmosphere immediately makes you feel like you are in some Al Capone gangster movie.

— 55 —
81LTD

UNITED
KINGDOM

Liverpool

81 Seel Street, Liverpool, L1 4BB

COCKTAIL
BAR

◆ TO VISIT BEFORE YOU DIE BECAUSE

The delicious chilli hot dogs and the speakeasy drinks
guarantee a unique experience.

81LTD is a typical speakeasy-style cocktail bar, well hidden on one of Liverpool's most popular streets (Seel Street) above Salt Dog Slim's, a bar known for its beer and American-style chilli hot dogs.

81LTD is open just at the weekends – by appointment only – but can be hired for private parties or cocktail classes. You cannot enter 81LTD without passing through Salt Dog Slim's. The perfect opportunity to have 'one of them chilli dawgs' …

— 56 —
THE ALCHEMIST

UNITED
KINGDOM

London
6 Bevis Marks, London, EC3A 7BA

COCKTAIL
BAR

◆ TO VISIT BEFORE YOU DIE BECAUSE

The bartenders boldly mix what no one has mixed before: molecularly inspired mixology.

The Alchemist in London is a 'link' in an inventive cocktail chain that has several venues in the United Kingdom. The bar's name refers to its use of molecular mixology. The Alchemist is located in the heart of London, a stone's throw from 30 St Mary Axe, known as the Gherkin. Its light-filled interior is modern and the cocktail menu very diverse, ranging from classics like the mojito to house-made drinks that spark the imagination. The Alchemist is proud of how it works magic with ingredients, often surprising and confusing tipplers. Rare ingredients, chemical reactions, cocktails served in refillable hip flasks ... anything goes. They also teach master classes, and their restaurant serves excellent food.

AQUA SHARD

UNITED KINGDOM	London The Shard, 31 St Thomas Street, London, SE1 9RY	COCKTAIL BAR

◆ TO VISIT BEFORE YOU DIE BECAUSE

You will remember the lavatory forever.

Aqua Shard, located on the 31st floor of the Shard, serves innovative British cuisine. The cosmopolitan establishment's restaurant, private dining rooms and spectacular three-floor atrium bar offer breathtaking views of the city.

The bar is open all day with no reservation needed and boasts a wide range of cocktails inspired by the botanicals you so often see in the worlds of gin and British tea. Aqua Shard lets you take in the London skyline from sunrise to sunset.

www.aquashard.co.uk

— 58 —
BEAUFORT BAR

UNITED
KINGDOM

London
The Savoy Hotel, 99 Strand,
London, WC2R 0EU

HOTEL BAR

◆ TO VISIT BEFORE YOU DIE BECAUSE
This bar is famed for its theatrical drinks and breathtaking art deco decor.

The Beaufort Bar in London's Savoy Hotel is famed for its theatrical drinks and breathtaking art deco decor. The drinks menu itself also appeals to the imagination, taking the form of a beautifully illustrated tunnel book that pays homage to the history of the Savoy. Chief bartender Kyle Wilkinson and bar manager Anna Sebastian created this menu, whose 20 cocktails each tell a different story about the hotel through the accompanying illustrations. The first one is about Fred Astaire dancing on the roof of the hotel. The story's cocktail, 'Under the Stars', mixes Woodford Reserve Bourbon and Rye, chestnut, champagne syrup, sherry blend and bitters. Other stories with respective cocktails include a bellboy's first day on the job, the hotel's relaunch in 2010 and the cocktail shaker that lies buried in the American Bar. The drinks' unique tastes and ingredients make you feel like you are part of the story. Hotel guests can buy the limited edition of this very special menu.

— 59 —
THE AMERICAN BAR

UNITED
KINGDOM

London
The Savoy Hotel, 100 Strand,
London, WC2R 0EZ

HOTEL
BAR

◆ TO VISIT BEFORE YOU DIE BECAUSE

The classics are outrageously high-quality. The senior bartender,
World Champion barista Martin Hudak, makes coffee cocktails
that you really must try.

The American Bar lives within one of the most prestigious hotels in the world, the Savoy. This hotel, located on the bank of the river Thames and within easy walking distance of the British Museum and the Royal Opera House, opened its doors in 1889 and since then scores of celebrities and dignitaries, including Sir Winston Churchill, Frank Sinatra and Katharine Hepburn, have stayed there. The American Bar is considered to be one of the world's best hotel bars, as evidenced by its winning first place in the prestigious 'World's 50 Best Bars' list in 2017. Head barman Erik Lorincz and his team have created a menu called 'Coast to Coast' that takes you on a virtual journey across Britain through its evocative drinks. They first closely examined different categories of drinkers and then composed the menu on the basis of their preferences. The bar's name refers to America's popular bar culture and the American Bar was, in fact, one of the first European bars to introduce American cocktails. In 2014, this London icon, in collaboration with Cocchi, launched its very own limited-edition vermouth onto the market. Cocchi's expertise and the American Bar's profound knowledge of mixology ensured a unique result.

— 60 —
CONNAUGHT BAR

UNITED
KINGDOM

London
Carlos Place, London, W1K 2AL

COCKTAIL
BAR

◆ TO VISIT BEFORE YOU DIE BECAUSE

One of the star cocktails is the Fleurissimo,
a tribute to Princess Grace of Monaco.

The Connaught Bar, located in the heart of London, not only offers glamour in a very trendy, supercosy interior, but even looks as if it was lifted right out of some famous film set. The bar's interior is inspired by English and Irish art from the 1920s, making it the ideal place for a stylish party. The bar belongs to the the Connaught hotel, but it has its own private entrance and serves non-resident guests. The owners are Italian, and their origins are reflected in the ingredients of the cocktails. The bar offers a successful combination of true classics and innovative home-made drinks. The cocktail menu is divided into sections based on the four elements: earth, water, wind and fire. One of the star cocktails is the Fleurissimo, a tribute to Princess Grace of Monaco, and the alcohol-free cocktails are of exceptionally high quality. Feeling hungry? Do taste the hot and cold canapés! Looking for an exclusive taste instead? The caviar is superb.

www.the-connaught.co.uk/restaurants-bars/connaught-bar

— 61 —
BLOOMSBURY CLUB BAR

UNITED KINGDOM	London	HOTEL BAR
	Bloomsbury Hotel, 16–22 Great Russell Street, London, WC1B 3NN	

◆ TO VISIT BEFORE YOU DIE BECAUSE

It is fascinating to see the bartenders at work from up close, even if there are only four stools at the bar.

From its lair within the Bloomsbury Hotel, the Bloomsbury Club Bar exudes pure English elegance: the soft leather Chesterfield chairs, the wooden panelling, the atmospheric lighting and the wide bookshelves loaded with spirits. This bar is inspired by the eponymous group of writers, artists and intellectuals from the early twentieth century, which included Virginia Woolf and her husband Leonard Woolf, Vanessa Bell, Clive Bell, Lytton Strachey, James Strachey, Duncan Grant and John Maynard Keynes. A cocktail has been named after each of the group's ten core members so you can sip a 'Virginia Woolf' or a 'Duncan Grant', for example. If there is no room inside, try the Bloomsbury Club Bar's enticing terrace.

— 62 —
CHRISTOPHER'S MARTINI BAR

UNITED
KINGDOM

London
Covent Garden, 18 Wellington Street,
London, WC2E 7DD

COCKTAIL
BAR

◆ TO VISIT BEFORE YOU DIE BECAUSE

Christopher's Martini Bar has the longest marble table
we have ever seen in a bar. Impressive!

Christopher's is undoubtedly one of today's finest American restaurants in London. If you fancy an aperitif before dinner or one for the road afterwards, stroll over to the Martini Bar on the ground floor. In this theatrical space you can savour creative cocktails as well as tasty food. The stars of the menu are, of course, the Martinis, divided into 'classic', 'contemporary' and 'decadent'. If you feel like stepping outside the box, order a 'Nutella Martini' with Stolichnaya Vanilla Vodka, cacao liqueur, cream and Nutella. If you would rather play safe, then 'The Original' Martini will be more up your street.

www.christophersgrill.com

— 63 —
GERMAN GYMNASIUM

UNITED
KINGDOM

London
King's Boulevard, Kings Cross,
London, N1C 4BU

COCKTAIL
BAR

◆ TO VISIT BEFORE YOU DIE BECAUSE

The cocktails based on Monkey 47 gin are a must-try,
including one with Fever-Tree Orange Ginger Ale foam.

German Gymnasium is a bar-restaurant located in the heart of King's Cross and a stone's throw from St Pancras Station. As its name suggests, it is set in a former gymnasium, although you will find it hard to imagine gymnastics competitions taking place here. German Gymnasium managed to carry off the titles of 'Best Restaurant in a Heritage Building', 'Best UK Restaurant' and 'Best Overall Restaurant' all in one year, 2016. On the ground floor you will find the Grand Café, which serves tasty brasserie food at all hours of the day. The Meister Bar's staff will fix up some excellent cocktails, and the intermediate floor hosts a private diner that looks out over the brasserie down below. Its menu, inspired by German, Austrian and Eastern European cuisine, is a nod to the building's German heritage. In short, you do not come here just for the cocktails, but also for the fabulous interior and the delicious food.

— 64 —
ARTESIAN

UNITED
KINGDOM

London
The Langham, London, 1C Portland Place,
London, W1B 1JA

HOTEL
BAR

TO VISIT BEFORE YOU DIE BECAUSE

◆ Everything here is special, even the ice, which is produced using the very latest technology. Artesian's ice is purer, colder and with a higher density, making it last longer and your cocktails cooler.

Artesian, part of The Langham hotel, was named after the original 110-metre-deep well under the hotel, and is a winner of the coveted 'World's Best Bar' accolade, creating classic and innovative cocktails. At Artesian you are looked after by head bartender Remy Savage and bar manager Anna Sebastian. Both arrived at Artesian in 2017: Remy from Paris's Little Red Door and Anna from The Savoy's Beaufort Bar. They have assembled a remarkable crew, including Ran Van Ongevalle, Bacardi's 2017 Legacy winner. But do not let the name-dropping deceive you; Artesian is not a snobby bar with airs or graces. The entire staff is as warm and welcoming as you could wish for. Artesian currently serves a menu of drinks inspired by your memories, called Artesian Moments. Have you ever thought about what your first day at school would taste like or your 18th birthday, and how they would compare with your 30th birthday? These are the life-defining moments that influenced Artesian's team. If this seems confusing, then you have just found yourself yet another reason to go and visit Artesian. Do not wait too long, though, as they might change the menu!

www.artesian-bar.co.uk

150 BARS YOU NEED TO VISIT BEFORE YOU DIE

— 65 —
THE GIBSON

UNITED
KINGDOM

London
44 Old Street, London EC1V 9AQ

COCKTAIL
BAR

◆ TO VISIT BEFORE YOU DIE BECAUSE

Gin, vermouth and other spirits are mixed in a unique way to
create both innovative and classic drinks.

The Gibson is a model of elegance that serves world-class cocktails. Vermouth, gin and other spirits are mixed in a unique way to create both innovative and classic drinks. The bartenders are great experimenters, often using pickled ingredients. The Gibson is owned by Marian Beke, former bar manager of the Nightjar, a popular nearby bar. The Gibson's manager is Rusty Cerven, an award-winning bartender who worked very successfully at the Connaught Bar for years. No wonder, then, that every cocktail served at the Gibson is a gem.
The menu lists 49 cocktails. The bar's signature cocktail, the 'Gibson', is a must-try made with Tanqueray, Mancino Secco and a home-pickled onion. The other 48 cocktails are presented on 12 pages, each one preceded by the Anglo-Saxon name of the month, like a calendar. The menu's common thread is clearly originality. The 'Grand Orient Express', for example, is a cocktail created with Glenfiddich 12-Year-Old Whisky infused with smoked litchi, roasted barley tea and carob syrup, fresh galangal root, lime juice, sugar apple and Korean bulgogi marinade. The bar's interior looks Edwardian thanks to the mirrors on the tables, the antique sofas and the vintage shakers. A piano provides the finishing touch.

— 66 —
SEXY FISH

UNITED
KINGDOM

London
Berkeley Square House,
Berkeley Square, London, W1J 6BR

COCKTAIL
BAR

◆ TO VISIT BEFORE YOU DIE BECAUSE

The Umami Martini, with its Belvedere vodka infused with umami (a butter made with no fewer than 24 ingredients), is an amazing experience.

After the hefty 20 million euros that went into its decor, Sexy Fish, a part of the Caprice Holding Group, looks more like a museum than a restaurant: a Damian Hirst mermaid dominating a lava-stone bar, an enormous crocodile, a gold ceiling, WCs with floor-to-ceiling marble, and one of the largest live coral-reef tanks in the world. To get in, you need to make a reservation weeks in advance, even with the three shifts and the almost 200 seats. Executive chef Ben Orpwood serves mainly Asian fish dishes, tataki, tempura, various grilled options and raw food. The shared-dining concept is immensely popular, and if you manage to secure a seat, you might even spot Johnny Depp. It is not only the interior and the dishes that are epic, but also the drinks. The bar boasts a huge collection of Japanese whiskies (the second-largest in Europe) and the cocktail menu is inspired by the world of fashion, art and design.

www.sexyfish.com

— 67 —
HYDE BAR

UNITED KINGDOM

London
Roseate House, 3 Westbourne Terrace, London, W2 3UL

HOTEL BAR

◆ TO VISIT BEFORE YOU DIE BECAUSE
The Hyde Bar has a superb range of Macallan whiskies.

The Hyde Bar is an establishment not to be missed. The elegant interior may be enjoyed while exploring the drinks menu with its rare whiskies – they have over 130 premium whisky varieties – and other spirits in their original, Prohibition-era bottles.

Every beverage on the list has some special quality, either because of the complexity of its production or the story behind the bottle. Words, however, are just words. The menu at this bar, with its collection of cocktails carefully created by the Hyde Bar's mixologists, is not something to read about, but to see with your own eyes.

UNITED
KINGDOM

London
109–113 Queen's Gate, Kensington,
London, SW7 5JA

COCKTAIL
BAR

TO VISIT BEFORE YOU DIE BECAUSE

◆ The setting is amazingly beautiful, complete with floor-to-ceiling wood panelling and magnificent crystal chandeliers. The live jazz performances are also quite something.

K Bar lies in the heart of one of London's most sought-after neighbourhoods, on the corner of two of its most iconic streets: Queen's Gate and Old Brompton Road. The bar's ambience is that of a typical English gentleman's club: oak panelling, cobalt-blue hues, velvet bar stools and dazzling chandeliers. The cocktails, too, are decadence at its purest, for example the 'King of Queen's Gate', with its Jameson Select Reserve whiskey, King's Ginger liqueur, lime, orange marmalade and rose syrup. Should you arrive at K Bar after dinner, the cocktail menu has various dessert cocktails in store for you.

— 69 —
JAILHOUSE BAR

UNITED
KINGDOM

London
The Courthouse Hotel Shoreditch,
335–337 Old Street, London, EC1V 9LL

HOTEL
BAR

◆ TO VISIT BEFORE YOU DIE BECAUSE
At this bar you can drink classic cocktails in the decidedly
non-classic surroundings of original jail cells.

The Courthouse Hotel Shoreditch is one of the most stylish hotels in Shoreditch. This boutique hotel, located within the former Old Street Magistrates' Court and police station, offers modern luxury with a historical twist. Its bar, appropriately named the Jailhouse Bar, is set in the police station's former cells. The brick walls, wooden panelling and subdued lighting offer a unique experience. A relaxing lounge during the day and a hip club at night, this is the formula that has made the Jailhouse Bar one of the most popular hotspots in London. Innovative cocktails as well as true classics adorn the menu. The 'Ball and Chain', for example, is a concoction of Sipsmith Sloe Gin, Cointreau, lemon juice and orange marmalade served with a shot of prosecco. Then there is a cocktail made with kumquat, bourbon and apple juice called the 'Liquid Cosh'. If you are still not convinced, then how about 'the Solitary' and its intoxicating mix of rum, lime juice, pure chocolate liqueur, red chilli and ginger beer? In addition to cocktails and other tasty beverages, you can also order cool street food.

MILK & HONEY

UNITED KINGDOM	**London** 61 Poland Street, Soho, London, W1F 7NU	COCKTAIL BAR

TO VISIT BEFORE YOU DIE BECAUSE

◆ The bartenders say they even count the number of times they shake or stir cocktails to ensure the perfect mix.

Floors full of surprises and delicacies submerged in a trendy, speakeasy atmosphere, Milk & Honey, a bar in London's Soho district, has become an institution since its 2002 inauguration. Milk & Honey's three floors boast a variety of bars and intimate corners, lounge areas and access to the most exclusive cocktails. All juices are hand-pressed and mixing glasses are frozen to -40°C to keep the drinks cool during the delicate preparation process. The bartenders say they even count the number of times they shake or stir cocktails to ensure the perfect mix. The ice is hand-cut from a twice-frozen block of mineral-water ice. This ice is colder and clearer, so cooling the cocktails without diluting them. The cocktail menu has some 30 beverages ranging from classics to contemporary combinations: more sophisticated than risky, but not to be missed. Milk & Honey is proud to be in the business of hunting rare bottles. Therefore, in addition to cocktails, the bar offers a collection of valuable wines, champagnes, whiskies, Armagnacs and other digestifs. One thing, though: Milk & Honey is a private club. Non-members can enter only by reservation until 11 p.m. For members and their guests the bar opens six nights a week until 3 a.m. In other words, if you want to enjoy the exclusive bar and cocktails, you will have to choose and reserve a Monday or Tuesday. Or quickly make new friends with a membership ...

UNITED
KINGDOM

London
58 St Martin's Lane, London, WC2N 4EA

COCKTAIL
BAR

◆ TO VISIT BEFORE YOU DIE BECAUSE

There are at least six different outrageously tasty sandwiches, which are ideal accompaniments to the locally brewed draught beer.

Mr Fogg's Tavern is anything but your usual cocktail bar. This Covent Garden venue with its Victorian interior is the perfect antidote to the city centre's hustle and bustle. Guests can enjoy a drink in the lively tavern on the ground floor or go upstairs to the quieter gin salon/cocktail lounge. In the tavern downstairs you can eat tasty stews and hearty pies, washing them down with a draught beer. Upstairs is where you sit back in an elegant salon complete with chaise longues, and sip a tipple selected from the best champagnes, more than 80 types of gin, or a small but remarkable range of wines and sherries. The cocktails bear amusing names (you will find them easier to pronounce before you have started drinking). The cocktail menu follows the seasons, so you will need to visit Mr Fogg's Tavern more than once. Moreover, in Mayfair you also have Mr Fogg's residence, the fictional home of Phileas Fogg, the protagonist in the Jules Verne novel *Around the World in Eighty Days*.

— 72 —
NIGHTJAR

London

129 City Road, London, EC1V 1JB

COCKTAIL
BAR

◆ TO VISIT BEFORE YOU DIE BECAUSE

This bar has made a name for itself through its eccentric presentations and tastes.

A favourite of many cocktail lovers, Nightjar has epitomised old-fashioned glamour since 2010. What makes it so exceptionally good are the sublime cocktails expertly combined with equally stellar live music. The cocktail menu is divided into four sections, each of which pays tribute to the glorious history of the cocktail: 'Pre-Prohibition' (1600–1918), 'Prohibition' (1918–1932), 'Post-war' (1940–2000) and 'Nightjar Signatures'. Of course, the bar team also accepts suggestions from its customers and offers a broad range of spirits served on the rocks or with premium mixers. Large groups can order Nightjar Sharing Cocktails, various types of punchbowls or delicious concoctions for eight people. Nightjar has only a few non-reservation tables, and they are assigned on a first-come-first-served basis. Considering the bar's no-standing policy, we definitely recommend making a reservation.

— 73 —
ORIOLE

UNITED
KINGDOM

London

Smithfield Markets, East Poultry Ave, London,
EC1A 9LH

COCKTAIL
BAR

◆ TO VISIT BEFORE YOU DIE BECAUSE

Oriole offers the perfect combination of beguiling decor, exciting drinks and
bites, and glowing hospitality.

The Oriole Bar is the brainchild of the
family behind the successful Nightjar
concept. Located in London's Smithfield
Markets, it opened in November 2015. Its
sumptuous setting is an oasis of warmth,
mystery and magic. Oriole offers the
perfect combination of beguiling decor,
exciting drinks and bites, and glowing
hospitality. In addition, there is a touch of
exoticism and an unparalleled programme
of live swing, jazz and blues. Sit down at
the bar or settle into one of the leather-
covered booths with spacious tables.
The bar team, headed by Luca Cinalli,
uses themes like travel and adventure
to compose a cocktail menu featuring
unusual creations from all over the world.
The Old World section refers to Europe
and Africa, and its selection honours these
regions' enormous diversity. Try the 'Forest
Sprite', a combination of gin, Arlette beer,
wormwood matcha and thaiberry tea. The
New World section takes you to America,
evoking a sense of discovery. Thus, the
'Prairie Horn' mixes bourbon with house
compost tea, prekese syrup and mustard
foam. Then there is the 'Orient', which
stands out for its boldness and daring. The
'Ryoan-Ji' is a blend of blue-rose milk,
Japanese whisky and seaweed syrup served
in a ceramic egg basket.

UNITED KINGDOM	London 252 High Holborn, London, WC1V 7EN	COCKTAIL BAR

◆ TO VISIT BEFORE YOU DIE BECAUSE

The finger food is well worth sampling. Be sure to order the delicious pata negra. And sometimes there is a theme bar set up in the courtyard, like a Hendrick's Gin bar in winter, for example.

This elegant jazz bar has the look of a real English gentleman's club and a very cosy feel. Scarfes Bar, with its more than 200 single malts and a rare specialisation in sloe gin, is a homage to famous British artist Gerald Scarfe. In fact, you can enjoy this well-known caricaturist's work through the drawings with which the bar's walls are adorned. While settling into one of the velvet armchairs in front of the fire, you can also admire the more than 1,000 antique books resting on the shelves. The cocktails are inspired by Scarfe's art, bringing his most famous works to liquid life. The seven-nights-a-week complimentary live music is yet another reason to pay this bar a visit.

www.scarfesbar.com

— 75 —
SHANGHAI BAR

UNITED KINGDOM

London
31 St Thomas Street, London, SE1 9RY

COCKTAIL BAR

◆ TO VISIT BEFORE YOU DIE BECAUSE

The bar has the ultimate recipe for a successful night out: a great view, delicious Asian cuisine and exquisite, original cocktails.

Hutong opened in 2013 and is located on level 33 of the Shard. This Asian restaurant draws its inspiration from the dishes formerly served in the imperial palaces of old Peking, expertly reflecting the subtleties of northern Chinese cuisine in its recipes. Its signature dishes include soft-shell crab, crispy lamb ribs and, naturally, roasted Peking duck, considered by many to be the best in London. But enough about food. Hutong has a fantastic bar called the Shanghai Bar that is simply *the* perfect place for before-or after-dinner cocktails. Some of them actually include ingredients employed in traditional Chinese medicine. Interestingly, the bar also uses many of the spicy herbs and ingredients from the restaurant's kitchen. For example, the 'Old-Fashioned Peking' cocktail is made with Hennessy cognac that has been infused with Peking duck meat for a week. It goes without saying that this cocktail is the ideal accompaniment for roasted Peking duck. A must-try!

69 COLEBROOK ROW

UNITED
KINGDOM

London

69 Colebrooke Row, London, N1 8AA

COCKTAIL
BAR

◆ TO VISIT BEFORE YOU DIE BECAUSE

There is a seasonal menu and many of the ingredients
are developed in a real research-and-development laboratory.

This cosy cocktail bar is owned by Tony
Conigliaro, a renowned mixologist, and
is reminiscent of an Italian café from the
1950s. The drinks here are both classic and
innovative. 69 Colebrooke Row is a popular
hangout with many chefs and foodies.

When none other than chef Heston
Blumenthal calls this bar revolutionary, you
know you will be served some incredibly
tasty and surprising drinks. The owner even
went as far as taking a perfumery course to
gain insights that would allow him to make
even better cocktails.

www.69colebrookerow.com

SKY POD BAR

UNITED KINGDOM	London 1 Sky Garden Walk, London, EC3M 8AF	COCKTAIL BAR

◆ TO VISIT BEFORE YOU DIE BECAUSE

The view in the summer when the sun goes down is unforgettable.

Sky Pod Bar, located in the iconic Sky Garden, is open all day, offering trendy food and drinks with an impressive view of the city. Its offerings range from breakfast and various sharing plates to hip cocktails, the most popular of which is the 'Smoked Negroni'. The intense aroma of this twist on the classic Negroni is provided by Tanqueray Gin, Campari, Cynar, Antica Formula and Laphroaig 10 Year Old. Its characteristic smoky taste comes from the Laphroaig whisky and the vermouth, which work together perfectly to balance the bitterness of the blend. Once mixed, the Negroni is aged in a wooden barrel for a few months in order to intensify the smoky, woody flavour. Definitely a must-try! On Thursday, Friday and Saturday evenings popular bands and DJs provide live music on the stage, so bring along your dancing shoes!

WAVE BAR

UNITED KINGDOM	**London** 17 Berkeley Street, Mayfair, London, W1J 8EA	**COCKTAIL BAR**

◆ TO VISIT BEFORE YOU DIE BECAUSE

You do not just 'have' some dim sums here; you have a dim sum eating experience. When making your dinner reservation, ask to have your aperitif at the bar, where you can enjoy old-fashioned drinks with hand-carved ice balls!

Park Chinois is an ode to the romanticism and etiquette of yore, perfectly combined with today's excitement. The menu lists mostly Chinese-inspired dishes, but created with progressive ingredients and techniques. As for the interior, a film set would pale in comparison with its sumptuous luxury and the impeccably dressed waiters and barmen. The Wave Bar matches Park Chinois's exacting standards effortlessly. Rare, exclusive drinks are served alongside cocktails mixed with the finest ingredients. Classics receive a modern twist, and the signature cocktails are not only creative, but also incredibly delicious.

www.parkchinois.com/wave-bar

ZTH COCKTAIL LOUNGE

UNITED KINGDOM	London The Zetter Townhouse, 49–50 St John's Square, London, EC1V 4JJ	HOTEL BAR

◆ TO VISIT BEFORE YOU DIE BECAUSE

It is hard to resist the tremendously savoury 'Turf Club',
a gin cocktail with grass!

The Zetter Townhouse, part of the Zetter Group, operates two hotels in London, one in Clerkenwell and another in Marylebone. Quality and hospitality are their top priorities, and the same goes for the Clerkenwell ZTH Cocktail Lounge. Its passion for quality cocktails clearly shows in the menu and in Tony Conigliaro's creations abounding with home-made bitters, infusions and other herbal blends. The lounge has a feeling of familiarity about it that reminds you of family visits to an eccentric aunt or grandmother, hence its name 'Wilhelmina'. The interior is cosy and inviting, making it is easy to let yourself sink into one of the comfortable sofas and sip gin and tonics for hours on end.

— 80 —
LE PARFUM

FRANCE

Montpellier
55 Rue de la Cavalerie, 34090 Montpellier

COCKTAIL
BAR

◆ TO VISIT BEFORE YOU DIE BECAUSE

Both the sophistication and presentation of the drinks
will have you thinking you are in Japan.

Many people will recognise the name of this Asian-oriented cocktail bar, inspired as it is by Patrick Süskind's masterful novel *Perfume: The Story of a Murderer* (1985). The bar's owners serve cocktails as 'perfumed' and diverse as the scents mentioned in the book. The cocktails are creatively combined with equally perfumed snacks called dim sum, a Cantonese speciality. The whole decor also has an Asian feel, providing quite an unusual experience. Make sure you don't miss it!

www.barleparfum.com

— 81 —
CITY SPACE BAR

RUSSIA	Moscow Swissotel Krasnye Holmy, Kosmodamianskaya Naberezhnaya, 52, building 6, Moscow	COCKTAIL BAR

TO VISIT BEFORE YOU DIE BECAUSE

The view of the city is nothing more than spectacular.

City Space Bar has something for everyone, from molecular drinks to classic cocktails. Its trump card, however, is the panoramic view of the city, located as it is on the 34th floor of the Swissotel. Behold Moscow from on high while sipping a fantastic 'Swiss Basil'. This cocktail, designed to celebrate the hotel's tenth birthday, is made with rum, fresh basil, fresh ginger, fructose, lime juice and Angostura bitters.

GERMANY	Munich	COCKTAIL BAR
	Rathausstraße 3, 20095 Hamburg	

◆ TO VISIT BEFORE YOU DIE BECAUSE

The Campari cocktails here are out of this world.

Charles Schumann, now aged 76, is the man behind Schumann's. He is a bar icon, but he is also a lot more. He worked as a model for the Baldessarini fashion label, appeared in various Boss and Campari advertising campaigns, published a number of books (*American Bar* sold no fewer than 300,000 copies). His first bar – Schumann's American Bar – opened in 1982 in Munich's Maximilianstraße. It quickly became very popular among authors, journalists and artists. In 2003, the bar moved to the Odeonsplatz, which is still its home today, gradually becoming a restaurant and bar where you can enjoy perfectly served cocktails as well as some excellent dishes. The bar prefers quality to quantity, focusing mainly on classics. Schumann himself composed the succinct cocktail menu, which reserves a place of honour for Campari. Next to Schumann's bar there is a small extra bar, Schumann's Camparino, which specialises in Italian drinks ranging from cappuccino to tasty wines. In 2013, following one of his creative ideas, Schumann opened a third bar, this time located right above Schumann's: Les Fleurs du Mal, a cocktail bar with just one table that measures a full nine metres.

www.schumanns.de

DIE GOLDENE BAR

GERMANY

Munich
Prinzregentenstraße 1, 80538 Munich

COCKTAIL
BAR

◆ TO VISIT BEFORE YOU DIE BECAUSE
This place is an absolute favourite with the locals.

The owner of Die Goldene Bar, Klaus Rainer, is well known in Germany. He became all the rage as a bartender, eventually opening his own Die Goldene Bar in Munich's Haus der Kunst in 2010. Since its inauguration, the museum pub has become a hotspot for people looking for quality cocktails. But cocktails and other drinks are not all you can get there: breakfast, lunch and dinner are also waiting for you. In 2012 *Drinks International London* included Die Goldene Bar in its list of the 'World's 50 Best Bars'. The bar's name refers to Karl Heinz Dallinger's wall paintings, which pay homage to the origin of spirits on a gold-coloured background. The interior of the bar harks back to the 1950s, with a chandelier that once adorned the Savoy in Zurich. The bar also has a rich history and a beautiful English garden with a spacious terrace that makes cocktail-sipping here even more enjoyable.

— 84 —
CANDELARIA

FRANCE

Paris
52 Rue de Saintonge,
75003 Paris

COCKTAIL
BAR

◆ TO VISIT BEFORE YOU DIE BECAUSE

The menu proudly boasts around 20 unique mezcals
and some 25 premium tequilas.

La Candelaria is located in Le Marais, Paris's trendiest neighbourhood. This taquería, where Mexican chef Luis Rendón serves genuine Mexican cuisine, has an almost clandestine bar in the back. Its menu lists around 20 unique mezcals and about 25 premium tequilas, in addition to a range of fantastic cocktails. Your first thought when entering here is 'Prohibition': wooden furniture, subtle candlelight and a mysterious ambience. The bar's interior was designed by several young artists, and the cocktails are served by real pros from the renowned Parisian cocktail scene.

www.candelariaparis.com

CASTOR CLUB

Paris
4 Rue Hautefeuille,
75006 Paris

FRANCE

COCKTAIL
BAR

◆ TO VISIT BEFORE YOU DIE BECAUSE

The subdued atmosphere and vintage American music provide the perfect background for a cosy get-together.

When you enter the Parisian basement where Castor Club is located, you are whisked away to a lodge in the middle of the Icelandic tundra. The subdued atmosphere and vintage American music provide the perfect background for a cosy get-together. Having a quiet chat is not all you can do here, however. If you are out on a weekend night and want a cool place to enjoy a quality drink, Castor Club is the place for you. Owner Thomas Codsi is passionate about his profession, and you can taste it in his cocktails. The menu features Prohibition-era classics such as the 'Fish House Punch', a potent mix of rum, cognac, apricot brandy, maraschino, lemon, green tea and champagne. Also highly recommended is a cocktail composed of mezcal, Louisiana Hot Sauce and Red Stripe beer. This is a hip joint where you can meet trendy locals and a discerning Parisian bar crowd.

— 86 —
LE BAR BOTANISTE

FRANCE

Paris
Shangri-La Hotel, 10 Avenue d'Iéna,
75116 Paris

HOTEL
BAR

◆ TO VISIT BEFORE YOU DIE BECAUSE

The bar's exclusive nature-inspired decor creates an ambience as herbal as the drinks, providing welcome relief from the hustle and bustle of France's capital.

Le Bar Botaniste is located in the Shangri-La Hotel in Paris, the former residence of Prince Roland Bonaparte. As its name implies, the bar focuses on unusual, botanically based spirits. The bar's exclusive nature-inspired decor creates an ambience as herbal as the drinks, providing welcome relief from the hustle and bustle of France's capital. Head bartender Clément Emery and his team have developed a menu with *génépi*, absinthe and chartreuse. But this does not mean you cannot have gin, chartreuse and extremely rare vermouths too. The drinks list features 15 different uniquely composed and impressively presented cocktails.

www.shangri-la.com/fr/paris/shangrila/dining/bars-lounges/le-bar

— 87 —
DIRTY DICK

FRANCE

Paris
10 Rue Frochot, 75009 Paris

TIKI
BAR

TO VISIT BEFORE YOU DIE BECAUSE

◆ The tiki cocktails rank among the best anywhere.

In Paris's somewhat rough but also very hip neighbourhood of South Pigalle, aka 'SoPi', lies Dirty Dick. This is a real tiki bar with cool bartenders who mix up the most fantastic tiki cocktails with spectacular names such as 'Cannibal's Dilemma', 'Le Zombie' or 'Don the Beachcomber.' The name Dirty Dick comes from the establishment's former use as a hostess bar from 1931 until a few years ago. Bamboo, flashy sunsets, wall-mounted animal heads, imposing totem poles: Dirty Dick is not averse to some retro kitsch. It also serves many of its drinks in extra-kitschy glasses, which is fun, but more important is what is in the glasses. Rest assured, the drinks here are sublime. Dirty Dick is a bar you visit to drink rum-based cocktails. If you would rather have your rum pure, Dirty Dick stocks some 140 different brands. When you are holding a Dirty Dick tiki cocktail, you will feel like a character in *Hawaii Five-O*.

— 88 —
LE BAR GEORGES V

FRANCE

Paris
Four Seasons Hotel,
31 Avenue George V, 75008 Paris

**HOTEL
BAR**

◆ TO VISIT BEFORE YOU DIE BECAUSE

This place is the embodiment of pure luxury: royal comfort, culinary pampering and magnificent Renaissance architecture.

The Four Seasons Hotel George V, located adjacent to the Champs-Elysées, is the embodiment of pure luxury: royal comfort, culinary pampering and magnificent Renaissance architecture. The bar of one of Paris's classiest hotels naturally had to meet the same high standards. Its interior includes Louis XVI furniture, an open fireplace and a library. Needless to say, the cocktail menu is sophisticated, featuring both classics and home-made creations. Going shopping in Paris? Then you absolutely have to enjoy a glass of champagne or a dry Martini here. Come and savour Paris's ambience and submerge yourself in luxury.

— 89 —
LITTLE
RED DOOR

FRANCE

Paris
60 Rue Charlot, 75003 Paris

COCKTAIL
BAR

◆ TO VISIT BEFORE YOU DIE BECAUSE

This bar became famous under the flamboyant Remy Savage, who is now in charge at the renowned Artesian in London.

As the name of this small, cosy bar implies, you enter through a little red door. At least, you usually do, because sometimes the door is locked, in which case you just use the one next to it. Once inside, you are welcomed by an extremely intimate ambience: flickering candlelight, snug corners, and affable bartenders. The creative cocktails are served in attractive vintage glassware. If you have particular tastes, let the bartender know and he will make something special that will completely surprise you. The Little Red Door is an absolute must-try in Paris, but bear in mind that it can get very busy at weekends and waiting lists are long.

www.lrdparis.com

— 90 —
LE BAR DU PLAZA ATHENEE

FRANCE

Paris
25 Avenue Montaigne, 75008 Paris

HOTEL
BAR

◆ TO VISIT BEFORE YOU DIE BECAUSE

This bar, located on Paris's prestigious Avenue Montaigne, combines the typically French classic style with the latest in hip bar technology.

Expect luxury, luxury and more luxury. This bar, located in the eponymous hotel on Paris's prestigious Avenue Montaigne, combines the typically French classic style with the latest in hip bar technology: an unlikely marriage, but one that is 'meant to be' and makes the Bar du Plaza Athénée one of the city's hotspots. The interior was designed by Patrick Jouin. The sculpted glass bar counter with high chairs is a real eye-catcher. The low leather sofas invite you to lean back and relax in style while, of course, sipping an elegant cocktail. The drinks list offers classic cocktails but with a clever added twist. How about Apple Martinis with home-made ice lollies and black mojitos? Given the bar's clientele, it naturally lists a wide range of champagnes and serves caviar and blinis with smoked salmon. All of this comes at a price, but then this is the bar where the rich and royal come to enjoy themselves.

— 91 —
SHERRY BUTT

FRANCE

Paris
20 Rue Beautreillis, 75004 Paris

COCKTAIL BAR

TO VISIT BEFORE YOU DIE BECAUSE

◆ Its attention to detail, relaxed atmosphere and intriguing menu make this bar an absolute must-visit.

Sherry Butt is the home of serious cocktails accompanied by trendy bar bites in an unpretentious neighbourhood close to the Bastille. Its attention to detail, relaxed atmosphere and intriguing menu make this bar an absolute must-visit. The name refers to a large barrel in which whisky is aged. It will come as no surprise, then, that the bar boasts quite an extensive whisky selection. Sherry Butt is the perfect place to hang out with friends, in part because so far it has not been swamped with tourists. The cocktail menu is written in chalk on the wall; once you have made your choice, you will be overwhelmed by the taste and finishing. Hip yet not intimidating, at weekends funky DJs add the finishing touch to Sherry Butt: a terrific place for a night out!

www.sherrybuttparis.com

HEMINGWAY BAR

CZECH REPUBLIC	Prague	COCKTAIL BAR
	Karolíny Světlé 279/26, 110 00 Prague	

◆ TO VISIT BEFORE YOU DIE BECAUSE

Every month the bar has its 'calendar cocktails', favourites that are served only during that month.

This bar's name immediately makes clear who inspired it. Ernest Hemingway was not only a famous writer and journalist, but also an assiduous bar patron, all over the world. The Hemingway Bar in Prague devotes much attention to this historical figure's favourite drinks, but absinthe still takes centre stage. Let the experienced bartender guide you in your choice of absinthe, because the drinks list features some truly rare gems. If you like rum, you will be pleased to know they have more than 200 different brands. Do try the 'rum-tasting experience' (you need to order in advance), which includes various rums combined with assorted nuts, chocolate and dried fruits. In addition to the usual big champagne brands, the Hemingway Bar offers bottles by small producers. The cocktails are expertly prepared with premium spirits and fresh ingredients. The Hemingway Bar puts a new twist on all-time classics.

— 93 —
THE JERRY THOMAS PROJECT

ITALY

Rome
Vicolo Cellini 30, 00186 Rome

COCKTAIL BAR

◆ TO VISIT BEFORE YOU DIE BECAUSE
They serve an exclusive vermouth with vanilla pods that you just *have* to try: the 'Vermut Del Vaniglia'.

If you know your way around the cocktail scene, you will certainly have heard of this bar. It became famous for only allowing customers to enter by giving a password previously obtained by answering a number of questions on the bar's website. Although the Jerry Thomas Project is located in the middle of the city centre near busy Piazza Navona in Campo de' Fiori, it is not easy to find, hidden as it is in a dark alley behind an even darker door. The bar has a speakeasy feel, no doubt because of the red walls, Chesterfield sofas and 1920s-style music and bartender attire. The drinks list is impressive: classics, home-made surprises, champagne cocktails that beat many others hands down, and much more. This bar will not make your heart beat faster if you are a vodka lover, because they do not serve any here, but they do brew their own, world-renowned 'Vermut Del Professore' vermouth as well as a gin, the 'Gin Del Professore'. The Jerry Thomas Project is an absolute must-visit for whoever sets foot in Rome! Start hunting for that password ...

www.thejerrythomasproject.it

SWEDEN	Stockholm	COCKTAIL BAR
	Hornsbruksgatan 24, 117 34 Stockholm	

◆ TO VISIT BEFORE YOU DIE BECAUSE

Linje Tio is renowned for its Sunday brunch and its own 'craft ice' programme.

The name of this cocktail bar, which literally means 'Line Ten', refers to the tram line that used to link the north of Stockholm (Värtahamnen) with the south (Hornstull). Located in Södermalm, the southern part of Stockholm's city centre, the Linje Tio restaurant brings back memories of the trams that once ran through the streets in this part of town. In order to attract as wide a clientele as possible, the restaurant-bar has made its menu very varied. The founders of this hip joint – Joel Söderbäck, Andreas Bergman and Robert Rudinski – looked for and found inspiration in the south of Europe. The mainly Mediterranean dishes can be perfectly combined, if you so desire, with their exceptional cocktails. Linje Tio is also renowned for its Sunday brunch and its own 'craft ice' programme.

www.linjetio.com

— 95 —
MR SIMON

ITALY

Udine
Secret address

COCKTAIL
BAR

◆ TO VISIT BEFORE YOU DIE BECAUSE

This is not 'just' a bar, but a creative and highly mysterious project by the renowned agency Visual Display.

This extremely mysterious bar is hidden behind a broom closet in an undisclosed restaurant somewhere in the city of Udine. What restaurant? That you will have to find out for yourself. In addition, to get in you need an access code that is obtained by phone reservation only. This creative project is the brainchild of Visual Display, an agency specialising in retail design and brand building. The bar's name refers to a fictional figure, 'Mr Simon', a mixologist who loves travelling and alchemy. The bar has only 25 seats, but once you manage to secure one, you are treated as if you are a special guest of the owner himself. You will get to drink cocktails you have never tasted before, and your every whim will be pandered to.

www.mrsimon.it

ITALY

Venice

Calle Vallaresso 1323,
30124 San Marco, Venice

**COCKTAIL
BAR**

◆ TO VISIT BEFORE YOU DIE BECAUSE

This bar is world famous for its excellent cicchetti and beef carpaccio.

Harry's Bar, located in Calle Vallaresso in San Marco, Venice, is one of the most famous bar-restaurants in the world. Bartender Giuseppe Cipriani opened the bar in 1931. It is known for its excellent cicchetti and beef carpaccio. In fact, Cipriani invented the latter dish, naming it after Renaissance painter Vittore Carpaccio because its colours reminded him of those in Carpaccio's paintings. Harry's Bar is renowned for serving one of the best cocktails in the world, the 'Bellini'. Its 'Dry Martini' is also internationally famous for its dryness. With its ratio of 15 parts gin to one part dry vermouth, it beats all its opponents effortlessly. The Martinis, served frosty-cold in shot glasses without any ice cubes, are prepared in advance and kept in the bar refrigerator until someone orders one. Many celebrities have frequented Harry's Bar. Ernest Hemingway, a regular, wrote the ending of *Across the River and into the Trees* here in 1950, even mentioning the bar several times in his book.

— 97 —
BAISER BAR

GREECE

Xanthi
Vasilissis Sofias 5, Xanthi, 671 00

COCKTAIL
BAR

◆ TO VISIT BEFORE YOU DIE BECAUSE

Its modern design with Greek undertones by architect Minas Kosmidis is absolutely high end.

If you love design, the Baiser Bar in northern Greece is the place for you. A decade ago, Thessaloniki-based architect Minas Kosmidis applied his magic touch to the bar, decorating it in his well-known funky, eclectic style. Kosmidis transformed it into a space that is totally what you would expect modern design with Greek undertones to look like.

Sober colours alternate with luxury materials such as walnut wood and marble, and custom-designed lighting above the Kartell counter literally puts the cocktails in a special light. At noon you can savour various speciality coffees and on weekends regular performances by DJs and other artists add to your delight. It can get quite busy in here, even during coffee hour ...

www.facebook.com/cafebar.baiser/

Daiquiri

Chill a coupette glass.
Fill a shaker with ice cubes
and the following:
→ 60 ml (1/4 cup) Plantation 3 Stars White Rum
→ 30 ml (2 tablespoons) lime juice
→ 20 ml (4 teaspoons) lime cordial
→ 10 ml (2 teaspoons) Falernum

Strain into the chilled glass.
Garnish with lime zest.

Emperor's Garden

Chill a coupette glass.
→ 50 ml (1/5 cup) Riesling wine
→ 15 ml (1 tablespoon) ginger syrup
→ 20 ml (4 teaspoons) Forest Dry Gin Autumn
→ 10 ml (2 teaspoons) plum wine
→ 10 ml (2 teaspoons) St Germain
→ 1 bar spoon (1.25 ml or 1/4 teaspoon) Yuzu

Stir for 15 seconds in a mixing glass with ice
cubes, strain, and serve in the chilled glass.
Garnish with a rose petal.

Gimlet

Fill a shaker with ice cubes, 75 ml (5 tablespoons) of Forest Dry Gin Summer, 15 ml (1 tablespoon) of fresh lime juice, and 15 ml (1 tablespoon) of lime syrup.
Close the shaker, shake hard for 25 seconds, double strain at the neck into a chilled coupette glass, and garnish with lime or lemon zest.

Gin and Tonic

Fill a long-drink glass with ice cubes and the
following:
→ 50 ml (1/5 cup) Bombay Sapphire gin
→ 150 ml (3/5 cup) Erasmus Bond Dry Tonic

Garnish with a slice of lime.

Grappa Sour

Chill a wine glass.
Pour a dash (0.625 ml or 1/8 teaspoon) of
egg white into a shaker, briefly shake very
hard and then fill the shaker with ice cubes
and the following:
→ 45 ml (3 tablespoons)
   Grappa di Barbera – Marolo
→ 20 ml (4 teaspoons) lime juice
→ 10 ml (2 teaspoons) orange cordial
→ 10 ml (2 teaspoons) sugar syrup

Serve in the chilled glass.

Mai Tai

→ 30 ml (2 tablespoons) Trois Rivières Blanc
→ 30 ml (2 tablespoons) Bacardi 8 Year Old
→ 10 ml (2 teaspoons) Overproof Rum
→ 20 ml (4 teaspoons) Cointreau
→ 25 ml (5 teaspoons) lime juice
→ 10 ml (2 teaspoons) Falernum
→ 2 bar spoons (2.5 ml or 1/2 teaspoon)
   almond cream
→ 2 ml (3/8 teaspoon) orgeat syrup
→ 1 dash (0.625 ml or 1/8 teaspoon) vanilla syrup

Shake with crushed ice.
Garnish with exotic flowers.

SWITZERLAND	**Zurich** Widder Hotel, Widdergasse 6, 8001 Zurich	HOTEL BAR

◆ TO VISIT BEFORE YOU DIE BECAUSE

If you ask, they will let you have your drink up on the roof terrace while looking out over the city.

Any visit to Zurich just *has to* include a stay at the Widder Hotel. This unique hotel consists of nine Mediterranean houses, their rooms chock-full of trinkets, antiques, contemporary artworks and design classics. The hotel also houses Zurich's best-known jazz clubs and, down in the cellar, another pearl, the Widder Bar. Its centrepiece is a curved wooden bar with a treasure trove of beverages, spirits and, especially, an impressive range of whiskies. With no fewer than 205 single malts to choose from, this is a true paradise for serious whisky aficionados. The cocktails, too, are top-quality; you will often find a whole encyclopedia of flavours in your glass. Hungry? The gourmet Widder Restaurant (15/20 Gault-Millau) certainly deserves a star. More than one, actually ...

— 99 —
SKY BAR

	Bangkok	
THAILAND	Lebua Hotel, 1055 Silom Road Bangrak, Bangkok, 10500	HOTEL BAR

◆ TO VISIT BEFORE YOU DIE BECAUSE

The round bar at the far end of the rooftop terrace is a perfect location for a glass of champagne with your loved one.

Sky Bar is on the 64th floor of the Lebua State Tower and is best known for its characteristic gold steel-and-concrete dome. This rooftop bar offers a stunning panoramic view of the Chao Phraya river and the enormous city of Bangkok with its eight million inhabitants. Sky Bar has made it to the Top 5 of the world's most unique bars on several occasions and was used as a film set for the film *The Hangover Part II* (2011). Not surprisingly, the 'Hangovertini', made with whisky, green tea liquor, green apple juice, Martini Rosso and rosemary-infused honey, is one of the most popular cocktails on the list. In summer the Poptails – a combination of cocktail and ice pop, or 'cocktaillolly' – are all the rage. Nothing beats the all-round view, however, which offers you the most wonderful sunsets in Bangkok.

— 100 —
BAMBOO BAR

THAILAND

Bangkok

Mandarin Oriental Hotel, 8 Oriental Avenue,
Bangkok, 10500

HOTEL
BAR

◆ TO VISIT BEFORE YOU DIE BECAUSE

The chef's taster – Oscietra caviar with sea urchins, potatoes
and champagne sauce – is heaven on earth.

The Bamboo Bar in the Mandarin Oriental is a shrine for music lovers and trendy people from all over the world, with live jazz on almost all week. The space itself has an exotic feel and a clubby ambience. This hotel bar has provided a getaway for those wishing to escape the hustle and bustle of the city since its inception in 1953. Not only are the music and vibe top-notch, but the cocktails are, too, and the award-winning bar team often draws inspiration from well-known jazz legends. All the 'Bamboo Bar Originals' are worth trying and have a permanent place reserved for them on the drinks list.

— 101 —
RED SKY

THAILAND

Bangkok
Centara Grand Hotel, 999/99 Rama 1 Road,
Pathumwan, CentralWorld 56F

HOTEL
BAR

◆ TO VISIT BEFORE YOU DIE BECAUSE

The DJ whips up a party atmosphere from Tuesday to Sunday.

Red Sky lies in the heart of Bangkok's vibrant Ratchaprasong shopping district, extending over two floors of the Centara Grand Hotel. The first of these, the 55th floor, it occupies completely, both inside and outside, and you can have something to eat and sip cocktails here. On the next floor, the bar takes up only the exterior part, but all of it, fully encircling the building. The view is phenomenal, and it is a wonderful place to have a drink while watching the sun go down and enjoy dinner under the stars. Red Sky has an extensive cocktail menu highlighted by 15 different Martinis and four signature Martinis. Other classic and contemporary drinks are also available, of course, and all of them may be accompanied by perfectly paired snacks.

www.centarahotelsresorts.com/redsky

— 102 —
ZOOM SKY BAR

Bangkok

THAILAND

6 Naradhiwat Rajanagarindra Road, Khwaeng Yan
Nawa, Khet Sathorn, Krung Thep Maha Nakhon 10120

HOTEL
BAR

◆ TO VISIT BEFORE YOU DIE BECAUSE

The live saxophone performances, the gorgeous view, the delicious finger food
and the drinks all combine into an irresistible 'cocktail'.

Discover another side of Bangkok while enjoying a breathtaking view of the city's bustling streets from 40 storeys high. You can also savour French dishes with an Asian twist and sample creative drinks. There are no bad spots here, because every seat offers an unobstructed panoramic view of the city. From 5.30 p.m. until 8.00 p.m. is happy hour, so you get two drinks for the price of one. You never have to reach deep into your pockets to have a fantastic evening at Zoom Sky Bar.

— 103 —
GOLD ON 27

UNITED
ARAB
EMIRATES

Dubai

Burj Al Arab Jumeirah Hotel, 27th Floor,
Burj Al Arab, Jumeirah Beach Road, Dubai

HOTEL
BAR

◆ TO VISIT BEFORE YOU DIE BECAUSE

Expect pure luxury, gold leaf and progressive drinks
that are unique in Dubai.

Gold on 27 in world-famous Burj Al Arab, Jumeirah, is definitely worth a visit. Expect pure luxury, gold leaf and progressive drinks that are unique in Dubai. Using premium brands and unusual ingredients, including saffron, truffles, goat's-milk cheese, charcoal and foie gras, the Gold on 27 mixology team has created an imaginative menu replete with contemporary twists, all named after local traditions and sayings.

www.goldon27.com

| UNITED ARAB EMIRATES | Dubai
JW Marriott Marquis Hotel,
Sheikh Zayed Road, Dubai | HOTEL BAR |

◆ TO VISIT BEFORE YOU DIE BECAUSE

Our favourite here is the 'Green Mountain Dynamite',
with Ketel One Citroen, cayenne pepper, maple bitters and maple syrup.

Vault has such a lot to offer along with the breathtaking view of Dubai. The highly skilled bar team will mix anything from the extensive menu of classics, classics with a twist, contemporary trends, 'healthier' cocktails and mocktails, whiskies paired with just the right cigars, and a whole array of gins and tonics. Every week, different themed evenings are organised. Tuesday night, for instance, is ladies' night, while Wednesday is reserved for gentlemen. The bar's interior is chic, classic and maybe a tad elitist, but then again, so is Dubai. A popular cocktail on the menu is the 'Deposit Box': Woodford Reserve, Cointreau, and orange and Angostura bitters that are aged together with ginger and cinnamon in oak barrels for at least two weeks. The bar's mixologists claim that in order to fully appreciate these cocktails, one must accompany them with a good cigar. Alternatively, you may prefer the 'Cocktails with Purpose' or the somewhat 'healthier' cocktails. Our favourite is the 'Green Mountain Dynamite', with Ketel One Citroen, cayenne pepper, maple bitters and maple syrup.

— 105 —
THE CHINNERY

CHINA

Hong Kong

Mandarin Oriental Hotel,
5 Connaught Road Central, Central, Hong Kong

**HOTEL
BAR**

◆ TO VISIT BEFORE YOU DIE BECAUSE

The Chinnery is the repository of one of the world's largest collections
of (rare) single malt whiskies.

The Chinnery in the Mandarin Oriental Hotel is a typical British restaurant in – yes! – Hong Kong. First opening its doors back in 1963, it took its name from British painter George Chinnery, who moved to Asia to work. The Chinnery offers a relaxed atmosphere and specialises in traditional British fare such as shepherd's pie, fish and chips and pork pies. You will also find yourself choosing from one of the world's largest collections of (rare) single-malt whiskies. If you fancy a cool beer, the Chinnery has various types on tap, serving them in silver tankards. Most of the cocktails are classic types, but we would not have expected anything else in such an establishment.

— 106 —
CASTELLO 4

CHINA

Hong Kong, Causeway Bay
4/F, Oliv, No. 15 Sharp Street East,
Causeway Bay, Hong Kong

COCKTAIL
BAR

◆ TO VISIT BEFORE YOU DIE BECAUSE

The decor will make you feel like you are in a science-fiction film. But wait until you have sampled the food and drinks: now that's extraterrestrial!

A genuine delight for the eye, Castello 4 is a luxury restaurant with bar located in the heart of Hong Kong. It was designed by Michael Liu and enjoys a reputation as a must-visit offering a very special food-and-drink experience. Although the bar lies inside a commercial building, the designer successfully created a world of his own where ultra-modern looks combine harmoniously with an intimate ambience. The original finishing of the place was retained and the concrete walls give it an authentic feel. A triangular geometric pattern was placed in front of the large windows, still letting in natural light but at the same time creating the illusion that you have escaped the outside world for a moment. You have to look for a reason not to visit this establishment. It has everything: fine Italian cuisine, exquisite cocktails, a designer interior and the promise of a unique experience.

CLUB QING

Hong Kong

CHINA

10/F, Cosmos Building, 8–11 Lan Kwai Fong,
Central, Hong Kong

COCKTAIL
BAR

◆ TO VISIT BEFORE YOU DIE BECAUSE

If you mention their Asta Morris whiskies, you will receive instant VIP treatment.

At Club Qing you will find more than 300 types of whisky, mainly from Japan: an extraordinary collection containing a number of exclusives that you will not find anywhere else. Not a connoisseur? They have more than 30 tasting sets for those wishing to discover the world of Japanese whiskies. Should you not be a whisky lover, then go for the specially selected wines from France, Italy and Africa. The drinks list also contains some signature cocktails, of course, but this cosy bar is still the perfect place for a fine or surprising whisky.

www.clubqing.com

— 108 —
DJAPA BAR

CHINA

Hong Kong , Wan Chai
Shops G18–20, G/F, Lee Tung Avenue,
200 Queen's Road East

COCKTAIL
BAR

◆ TO VISIT BEFORE YOU DIE BECAUSE

The plates of crispy porquinho – pork, coconut confit, cinnamon apples,
kinome and spicy jam – are a must.

Djapa Bar lies in Wai Chang, in the heart of Hong Kong. It is a fairly new bar, but one that is still guaranteed to provide a unique experience. The interior playfully combines typical Japanese art and colourful Brazilian wall paintings. You can enjoy exceptional fusion cuisine on the first floor, and then go up one level and sit at the bar. Brazilian-inspired cocktails alternate with over 300 types of exclusive Japanese whiskies as well as a selection of fine Japanese sakes. The kitchen, too, combines the finesse and freshness of Japanese cuisine with the bold and hearty flavours of Brazil.

www.lecomptoir.hk/djapa/

185

— 109 —
DR FERN'S GIN PARLOUR

CHINA

Hong Kong

Shop B31A, First Basement Floor,
Landmark Atrium, 15 Queen's Road, Central, Hong Kong

COCKTAIL
BAR

◆ TO VISIT BEFORE YOU DIE BECAUSE

This theme bar has been conceived like a classic pharmacy, with staff wearing white jackets and 'patients' taking their pick from no fewer than 250 types of gin.

As its name rightly suggests, this theme bar serves a fantastic gin and tonic. It is conceived like a classic pharmacy, with staff wearing white jackets and 'patients' taking their pick from no fewer than 250 types of gin. Dr Fern, an eccentric doctor, became fascinated by the therapeutic effects of botanicals and decided to combine them with gin. The gin and tonics here are prepared in Collins glasses, with the ice being added at the end, right before serving. Like the good doctor, an eccentric way of presenting a gin and tonic, but this does not necessarily make it less good. The other cocktails, too, are made with fresh ingredients daily, so the menu is different each day. Definitely recommended for every self-respecting gin lover!

www.drfernshk.com

— 110 —
J. BOROSKI

CHINA

Hong Kong
17/F, Chinachem Hollywood Centre,
1–13 Hollywood Road, Central, Hong Kong

COCKTAIL
BAR

◆ TO VISIT BEFORE YOU DIE BECAUSE

There is no menu here. You determine what you are going to drink by telling the bartenders your preferences.

Famed bartender Joseph Boroski is the man in charge in his namesake bar. He has made it so exclusive that you need an invitation to get in. In other words, if you want to sample Boroski's equally exclusive cocktails, you had better start making friends in Hong Kong. But before you can do any of this, you first have to successfully locate the entrance.

Once inside, the curved bar will blow you away. There is no menu here. You determine what you are going to drink by telling the bartenders your preferences with regard to ingredients or tastes. Using their skill and creativity, they will conjure a custom-made, magical potion into your glass.

— 111 —
LOBSTER BAR
AND GRILL

Hong Kong

CHINA

Shangri-La Hotel, Supreme Court Road, Level 6,
Pacific Place, Central, Hong Kong

HOTEL
BAR

◆ TO VISIT BEFORE YOU DIE BECAUSE

As the name implies: try the delicious lobster dishes here.

For a long time the Lobster Bar, located in the Shangri-La Hotel, was your typical hotel bar focused on classic cocktails. At the end of 2017, however, bar manager Anne-Sophie Cross and head bartender Paolo De Venuto created a completely new cocktail menu, which they divided into 'The Past', 'The Present' and 'The Future'. Ten new signature cocktails adorn the menu, and each and every one of them is worth sampling. Not all on the same night, of course ... Adventurers will find the 'Legacy' to their liking: Chivas Regal, vetiver (essential oil), mango and a home-made horchata blend of cashew nuts, rice, sugar and water. The crowd pleaser? 'The Taste of Ling', made with Beefeater 24 Gin, ginger, vanilla and elderflower. The atmosphere at the Lobster Bar is relaxed, with a dash of luxury. The classy interior features a huge mahogany bar, comfortable seats, floor-to-ceiling windows and two impressive aquariums. As the bar's name implies, they also serve delicious lobster dishes.

www.shangri-la.com/hongkong/islandshangrila/
dining/restaurants/lobster-bar-grill

— 112 —
MO BAR

Hong Kong

15 Queen's Road Central, Central, Hong Kong

TO VISIT BEFORE YOU DIE BECAUSE

The world-class tea-based drinks they serve here are definitely worth a try.

Mo Bar is renowned for its superb cocktails and organic dishes. This hotel bar welcomes you from breakfast till noon, when a unique selection of sandwiches and pastries is served. As the sun goes down in the evening, the setting of the place changes. Every night the new DJs spin their songs in this enticing space, which was conceived by famous designer Adam Tihany. Everything looks sophisticated, up to and including the guests and drinks.

www.mandarinoriental.com/hong-kong/the-landmark/
fine-dining/bars/mo-bar

— 113 —
OPHELIA

Hong Kong , Wan Chai

CHINA

Shop No. 41A, 1/F The Avenue, 200 Queen's Road East,
Lee Tung Street, Hong Kong

COCKTAIL
BAR

◆ TO VISIT BEFORE YOU DIE BECAUSE

The themed evenings, when service, dress, and decoration
become one, are a sight to behold.

Ophelia's interior, inspired by Hong Kong's rich and lively culture, is the brainchild of architect Ashley Sutton, who has created a surprising universe for the bar's guests. You access the bar through an exotic-bird shop (yes, an exotic-bird shop). Once inside, you will be floored by the luxury furniture, 600,000 hand-painted tiles and state-of-the art metalwork making up the fabulous interior. But the main theme here is peacocks. You see them everywhere in the decor, even in the smallest details, creating the ultra-luxurious feel that pervades the place. The drinks are equally colourful and exotic. The bar's signature cocktails include The Opium Cage, a combination of Tequila Ocho Blanco, homemade watermelon syrup, rhubarb cordial and lime juice and The Muse fuses with Nusa Cana Rum, Pineapple juice, Orgeat syrup, lemon juice and cassis liqueur.

— 114 —
OTTO E MEZZO
BOMBANA

CHINA

Hong Kong

Shop 202, Landmark Alexandra, 18 Chater Road,
Central, Hong Kong

COCKTAIL
BAR

◆ TO VISIT BEFORE YOU DIE BECAUSE
If you want to be served the world's best wines, this is the place to come to.

This bar is the typical Italian venue where Negronis and Martinis reign supreme. It is named after a 1963 film by director Federico Fellini and serves the world's best wines. The bar is located in the middle of the eponymous restaurant where chef Umberto Bombana, famous for his truffle dishes and his hospitality, prepares Michelin-level food for you. The restaurant, in turn, is tucked inside the Alexander House, overlooking Chater Road: place in which to catch your breath and disconnect from the hustle and bustle of the city.

— 115 —
PLEASE
DON'T TELL

CHINA

Hong Kong
15 Queen's Road Central, Central, Hong Kong

HOTEL
BAR

◆ TO VISIT BEFORE YOU DIE BECAUSE
**Ask the head bartender a question about a spirit or trendy bar bite
and he will immediately entertain you with a story.**

Please Don't Tell or, in short, PDT, is the long-awaited speakeasy of the eponymous bar in New York. Head bartender Adam Schmidt first earned his stripes in New York and now handles the shakers in Hong Kong. His knowledge and skills go way beyond mixing up drinks: ask him a question about a spirit or trendy bar bites and he will immediately entertain you with a story.

After its success as a pop-up in Hong Kong in 2016, the bar has now permanently settled above MO Bar in the Landmark Mandarin Oriental. A secret phone booth provides access to the cosy PDT. Its cocktail menu may not be extensive, but quality-wise it is up there with the best. Try the cocktail-hotdog combination and be amazed!

www.mandarinoriental.com/hong-kong/the-landmark/
fine-dining/bars/pdt

— 116 —
QUINARY

CHINA

Hong Kong
56–58 Hollywood Road, Central, Hong Kong

COCKTAIL
BAR

◆ TO VISIT BEFORE YOU DIE BECAUSE

At Quinary expect the unexpected, like molecular cocktails that
will provide you with an exceptional experience.

At Quinary expect the unexpected, like molecular cocktails that will provide you with an exceptional experience, which is what you would expect from a bar that has been likened to Spain's former El Bulli restaurant, but in liquid form. Under Antonio Lai's leadership, the bar team does everything it can to surprise tipplers, serving cocktails of unprecedented quality that will baffle your senses. Just looking at the cocktail you have chosen will make you go 'wow'. Sample it and you will be totally blown away. Quinary's long bar stretches all the way to Lai's laboratory, with its rotary evaporator and all manner of ingenious equipment. Whatever else you do, make sure you try the signature 'Earl Grey Caviar Martini' with its Cointreau, Ketel One Citroen Vodka, elderflower syrup and Earl Grey caviar. Or perhaps you will be one of the lucky few to enjoy the 'A Walk in the Clouds' cocktail, of which only ten are made per day.

— 117 —
STOCKTON

CHINA

Hong Kong
32 Wyndham Street, Central, Hong Kong

COCKTAIL
BAR

◆ TO VISIT BEFORE YOU DIE BECAUSE

The roast-beef sandwich is truly delicious.

Stockton is pure rock 'n' roll, complete with oil paintings of David Bowie and Bill Murray, depicted as generals, hanging on the wall. The playfulness of the interior is reminiscent of chaotic punk. The cocktail menu is just a bit less chaotic. The 'Minds Undone' series pays homage to the great writers of our time and other inspirational figures behind Stockton's DNA. The 'Hidden Lady', for example, is inspired by Truman Capote and combines Ketel One Vodka with sake, apricot, orange sherbet, lime, mace, verbena syrup and house-made orange bitters. This bar is is not easy to find, hidden as it is in an alley just off Wyndham Street. Look for a short flight of stairs and set foot in this somewhat atypical, but definitely must-visit, cocktail bar.

INDIA	Jaipur Narain Niwas Palace Hotel, Kanota Bagh, Narain Singh Road, Jaipur, Rajasthan, 302004	HOTEL BAR

◆ TO VISIT BEFORE YOU DIE BECAUSE

The Palladio's unique interior is totally in line with the style of the local people and area.

This magical bar will have you thinking you are Alice in Wonderland. Bar Palladio sits within the grounds of the Narain Niwas Palace Hotel in Jaipur. You enter through a garden and are promptly welcomed by a group of peacocks. Settle into one of the lounge tents outside, or step into the lavishly decorated bar and enjoy the exquisite Italian cuisine and sumptuous cocktails. Bar Palladio has definitely succeeded in introducing the Italian *aperitivo* to Jaipur, offering an extensive menu ranging from Crisp Martini to Negroni, from prosecco to spritz.

www.bar-palladio.com

— 119 —
ROCK BAR

Jimbaran

BALI
INDONESIA

Ayana Resort & Spa, Jl. Karang Mas Sejahtera, Jimbaran, Kuta Sel., Kabupaten Badung, Bali, 80364

HOTEL
BAR

◆ TO VISIT BEFORE YOU DIE BECAUSE

Thanks to the location, among the rock formations along the coast of Jimbaran, even a glass of water becomes special here.

Rock Bar has as its stage the Indian Ocean and the rock formations along the coast of Jimbaran. Guests fly to the island specifically to sample the bar's signature cocktails and its magical ambience. They are especially fond of the Martini cocktails, including the 'Punch Rock', 'Rockberry Martini' and 'Spa on the Rock'. The cocktails were designed by international bar consultant Sebastien Bonnefoi, who mixed imported liqueurs with local fruit, herbs and spices.

www.ayana.com/bali/ayana-resort-and-spa/
eat-and-drink/venues/rockbar

— 120 —
AER LOUNGE

INDIA

Mumbai
Four Seasons Hotel, 1/136, 34th Floor,
Dr E. Moses Road, Worli, Mumbai

**HOTEL
BAR**

◆ TO VISIT BEFORE YOU DIE BECAUSE

**The location and views will make you think
you are on board a modern cruise ship.**

Admire the panoramic city and sea views and dream away underneath the endless ceiling of sky and stars at AER, Mumbai's highest bar. This modern, futuristic open-air lounge occupies the whole roof of the Four Seasons Hotel, drawing large crowds who come to enjoy its clubby ambience and lively music. The cocktail menu leaves nothing to be desired, either, but what you really come here for is the view. A must for the more adventurous cocktail drinker is undoubtedly the 'Fired Up', a mix of whisky, mint, pineapple and jalapeños.

— 121 —
CHARLES H. BAR

SOUTH
KOREA

Seoul
Four Seasons Hotel, 97 Saemunan-ro
Jongno-gu, Seoul

HOTEL
BAR

◆ TO VISIT BEFORE YOU DIE BECAUSE

The bar serves the 'Panacea' cocktail: Dominican white rum
and a very special ingredient, Chrysanthemum tincture.

This hotel bar is named after legendary American writer Charles H. Baker, Jr, who spent his life in search of the perfect drink. This speakeasy bar, located in the basement of the Four Seasons Hotel in Seoul, has a cocktail menu that truly appeals to the imagination. Barman Lorenzo Antinori takes you on a trip to the locations visited by Baker, dividing the menu into four sections: 'New York 1915', 'Manila 1926', 'Hong Kong 1932', and 'Cuba 1933'. His creations are either inspired by the writer's books or by the locations themselves. Try the 'Wellington Tea Punch' with its milk-washed Caribbean rum, Pu-erh tea, pear miso, elderflower and perilla. The menu also features cocktails by bartender friends from all around the world.

www.fourseasons.com/seoul/dining/lounges/charles_h

203

— 122 —
SPEAK LOW

◆ TO VISIT BEFORE YOU DIE BECAUSE

One of the leading bartenders at Speak Low is Faye Chen, who also participated in the Bacardi Legacy competition. Make sure you sample his 'Gold Fashioned' cocktail.

Speak Low is a speakeasy in the heart of Shanghai that really highlights the concept's illustrious character. It is directed by Japanese master mixologist Shingo Gokan, whose prowess and creativity ensure classy, perfectly mixed cocktails. The entrance to Speak Low is behind a traditional bookcase in Ocho Bar Tools, a shop selling bartending equipment. A sort of tunnel leads you to the first secret bar. Here you can drink traditional cocktails in a New Yorkish ambience. To get to the second bar, take the stairs to the next floor and scan the wall for a map. Once you have found it, press the city where Speak Low is located, and the sanctuary is yours to enter. This smaller, cosier bar serves exotic cocktails. Shouting is not allowed and there are just 20 seats. Most people's special speakeasy experience will end here, in the second bar, but there is more ... Go up yet another staircase (who would expect to find a third bar behind an 'Employees Only' sign?) and you will discover a Japanese whisky bar. Only a handful of lucky regulars are allowed in here, though.

— 123 —
28 HONGKONG STREET

SINGAPORE

Singapore
28 Hongkong Street, Singapore, 059667

COCKTAIL BAR

◆ TO VISIT BEFORE YOU DIE BECAUSE
Several of the drinks have been named after popular rappers, and hiphop classics sound from the loudspeakers.

This bar is one of the best drinking establishments in Singapore. Located on the ground floor of an old shophouse, 28 Hongkong Street opened its doors discreetly in 2011 and is as mysterious today as it was back then: no marketing, no website, no social-media presence. And yet, 28 Hongkong Street has grown into a frontrunner in the cocktail world. Expect to find a sophisticated interior with a classy black marble bar. What will have you coming back, however, is not the interior but the cocktails. The drinks in this bar scoff at the mainstream and are brimming with urban swag. Several of the drinks have been named after popular rappers, and hiphop classics sound from the loudspeakers. In short, this an ultra-hip bar with ultra-hip cocktails.

— 124 —
ATLAS BAR

SINGAPORE

Singapore
600 North Bridge Road,
Parkview Square, Singapore

COCKTAIL
BAR

◆ TO VISIT BEFORE YOU DIE BECAUSE

The magnificent collection of spirits, which includes all of
Jacques Selosse's cru champagnes, is truly unique.

Atlas graces the ground floor of Parkview Square, an iconic building in Singapore's Bugis neighbourhood. Yet this bar will make you feel as if you are in contemporary New York. Not in a speakeasy way, but with a certain light elegance. Atlas Bar, headed by Roman Foltán, is known for its sophisticated cocktails and its gin and champagne collections, which took more than two years to compile and contain true treasures. In addition to champagne and gin, Atlas also boasts exceptional wine (50,000 bottles) and whisky (10,000 bottles) collections gathered from the private collection of C.S. Hwang, the founder of the Parkview Group. The drinks list is divided into 'The Golden Age', 'The Gilded Age' and 'The Crazy Age'. Foodies are suitably pampered, too, by executive chef Daniele Sperindio, who prepares dishes using skills that he has acquired in Michelin-starred restaurants all over the world.

— 125 —
EMPLOYEES ONLY

SINGAPORE

Singapore
112 Amoy Street,
Singapore, 069932

COCKTAIL
BAR

◆ TO VISIT BEFORE YOU DIE BECAUSE
Many expats go there at the weekend, and they like to throw a great party.

Employees Only in Singapore is the second branch of the legendary eponymous New York cocktail bar. Located in a renovated shopping centre on Amoy Street, it takes you back to Prohibition-era New York. At the time of the bar's inauguration in 2016, the menu consisted of 17 cocktails copied from the main Manhattan bar but made with local, fresh ingredients. Things have evolved since then and traditional Asian tastes have now been integrated in the menu: the 'Mata Hari' cocktail, for example, blends Pierre Ferrand 1840 Cognac with pomegranate juice and Italian vermouth infused with typical local botanicals. The food here is also excellent: the truffled grilled cheese with parmesan fries and the famed EO dry-aged burger definitely deserve your attention. As in the main New York branch, patrons still present near closing time are served bowls of hot chicken soup. This bar is anything but pretentious. It just offers very good products, both in your glass and on your plate.

www.employeesonlysg.com

TIPPLING CLUB

SINGAPORE

Singapore
38 Tanjong Pagar Road,
Singapore, 088461

COCKTAIL
BAR

◆ TO VISIT BEFORE YOU DIE BECAUSE

In 2017 the Tippling Club received the 'Best International Restaurant Bar' award from Tales of the Cocktail, a renowned cocktail festival in New Orleans. It also serves a divine pork collar with cinnamon-infused dashi.

In 2013 the Tippling Club moved from Dempsey Hill to its current premises with its ultra-modern test kitchen. The food here is fabulous. Owner and chef Ryan Clift likes to experiment and is no stranger to molecular gastronomy. If you want to sample his culinary creations, then do ask for the full menu. If, on the other hand, you want to enjoy a nice drink, the cool bar is waiting for you. The cocktails are as experimental as the food, and there is such a wide variety that everyone is bound to find something to their liking. Absolute highlights are 'Baby', which incorporates milk, vanilla, apricot, honey, citrus and gin, and 'Indulge', with its cacao nibs, strawberries, and bourbon.

— 127 —
GIBSON BAR

Singapore
2nd Floor, 20 Bukit Pasoh Road,
Singapore, 089834

◆ TO VISIT BEFORE YOU DIE BECAUSE
The Monday and Tuesday raw-oyster happy hours are simply awesome.

The Gibson Bar pays homage to those who step outside the box. In other words, here you can name anything you want and it will be shaken or stirred for you. The bar is named after a true classic, the 'Gibson'. And just like the Gibson cocktail – a drink for people with discerning taste – the Gibson Bar is not afraid to drop the seriousness every now and then. Naturally, you cannot go to the Gibson without having a 'Gibson'. A mix of Tanqueray Gin, Ginjo Sake Vermouth, pickled onion, pickled ginger and smoked quail egg, this is a cocktail for daring individuals.

The drinks list – divided into 'World Collaboration Menu', 'Elevated Classics' and 'Inspired by People, Time & Place' – will generally appeal to connoisseurs in search of variety. Whether you want to sip a drink on your own or prefer to party with friends, the Gibson is certain to please even the most demanding of tipplers. Groups can enjoy different punchbowls, including the 'Go Bananas Punch' with banana-infused Monkey Shoulder Scotch, Nardini Rabarbaro, Ardbeg 10 Years Old Scotch Whisky, Brooklyn Lager and chocolate bitters. In addition to cocktails and its other offerings, the Gibson serves a small selection of raw seafood and snacks.

SINGAPORE

Singapore
101 Amoy Street,
Singapore, 069921

COCKTAIL
BAR

◆ TO VISIT BEFORE YOU DIE BECAUSE

Many of the cocktails are garnished with herbs or flowers from the Citizen Farm.

The king of classic cocktails? Jigger and Pony in Singapore. The bar was named after the 'jigger', a measuring device used when making cocktails. As for the 'pony', it is a narrow glass in which cocktails are stirred. In the nineteenth century, cocktail recipes were called either 'jiggers' or 'ponies', depending on how they were prepared. The menu appeals to both seasoned and novice cocktail drinkers. Out with friends? No problem, they serve several potent punchbowls. The bar provides all of this in a relaxed but still lively decor that invites you to linger just a little too long.

— 129 —
LONG BAR

SINGAPORE

Singapore
Raffles Hotel, 1 Beach Road,
Singapore, 189673

HOTEL
BAR

◆ TO VISIT BEFORE YOU DIE BECAUSE

As well as visiting the bar, take some time to wander through the hotel
and admire the wonderful fresh flower arrangements.

The Long Bar is the hotel bar of the world-famous Raffles Hotel. It is also where the legendary 'Singapore Sling' was first created in 1915 by bartender Ngiam Tong Boon. The 'Singapore Sling' is a primarily gin-based cocktail with pineapple juice as its main ingredient, combined with grenadine, lime juice and DOM Bénédictine. Cherry brandy and Cointreau are added to give the drink its nice, pink colour. In early twentieth-century colonial Singapore, the Raffles Hotel was the meeting place for the local community and the Long Bar the place for a pleasant drink. Women were not allowed to drink alcohol in those days, and Ngiam had the brilliant idea of designing a cocktail whose pink colour made it look like simple fruit juice. Needless to say, the 'Singapore Sling' was an instant hit among female guests.

— 130 —
MANHATTAN

	Singapore	
SINGAPORE	Regent Hotel, 1 Cuscaden Road, Level 2, Regent, Singapore, 249715	HOTEL BAR

◆ TO VISIT BEFORE YOU DIE BECAUSE

The bar serves a barrel-aged Michter's 'Manhattan'. Order one and, if you are lucky, the bartender will let you accompany him to the glass supply room.

Since April 2014, there has been a bar on the second floor of the Regent Hotel in Singapore: a bar that exemplifies timeless elegance and which will take you on a trip down memory lane, a trip that leads to nineteenth-century New York. This bar is called Manhattan. Its manager, Philip Bischoff, is a first-class professional, which is reflected in what you can both see and taste at his bar. It also has the world's first in-hotel rickhouse, where more than 100 oak barrels of various spirits lie ageing. Right in front of the rickhouse is the ingredients room with jars upon jars of maturing and fermenting herbs, fruit and botanicals. The bar bites, too, are gastronomical gems of remarkably

high quality. Take the 'Ziti Pot', made with Italian pasta, asparagus and truffle cream. The cocktail menu's 20 artisanal drinks will take you on a trip through five eras of New York. All-time classic cocktails are redefined and innovative new mixes created. Thus, the 'Ultimate Palavra' pays homage to this classic cocktail with its own mix of Maracatu Cachaça, Mancino Secco, yellow Chartreuse, lemon, citrus and mango tea syrup, while the 'TKH' offers a totally new experience combining Michter's US*1 Straight Rye, Amaro Averna, Knickerbocker Beer Syrup and Angostura bitters. Manhattan ranked seventh in the 2017 'World's 50 Best Bars' list and has been crowned the best bar in Asia.

OPERATION DAGGER

Singapore

7 Ann Siang Hill, #B1-01,
Singapore, 069791

◆ TO VISIT BEFORE YOU DIE BECAUSE

Operation Dagger serves the 'Kakigori', a beautifully presented outrageous cocktail of distilled Matcha tea, white chocolate, vanilla and melon.

Operation Dagger does the word 'clandestine' proud. This basement bar is hidden in a back alley at the junction of Club Street and Ann Siang Hill. Its entrance is so inconspicuous that even the building it is in does not have a name. The glass door with illegible scribbling and the unwashed floor lead to an equally dirty staircase that takes you further down, but it is especially the smell of burnt herbs that hits you first. What goes on in the basement, however, is pure magic. Headed by Luke Whearty and Aki Nishikura, the bar bathes in a haze of innumerable lightbulbs and enigmatic wall drawings. Given the exceptionally high quality of the duo's multi-sensory concoctions, it will surprise no one that Operation Dagger has already carried off numerous awards.

www.operationdagger.com

SMOKE & MIRRORS

	Singapore	
SINGAPORE	1 St Andrew's Road, Singapore, 178957	COCKTAIL BAR

◆ TO VISIT BEFORE YOU DIE BECAUSE

The cocktails are unbelievably creative, such as the one made with cacao-infused vodka, sweet vermouth and coconut nectar, which is served in … a flowerpot.

Smoke & Mirrors, located on the top floor of the National Gallery art museum, will have you enjoying both cocktails and an incredible view of Marina Bay. Upon entering you are struck by the stunning bar as well as the seamless transition from the outdoors to the indoors. The interior is dominated by woods, copper tones and warm lighting. The bartenders' discreet but engaging service reflects the personality of Smoke & Mirrors. The cocktail list is, to say the least, imaginative. Yugnes Susela is known for his eagerness to push the limits. The menu contains many culinary tricks. Yugnes likes to tease guests with difficult-to-eat garnishes such as eggcups ('Mighty Duck' cocktail) and edible stones ('Smoke & Mirrors' cocktail)! You really have to see and taste the cocktails to believe them.

www.smokeandmirrors.com.sg

Tel Aviv

ISRAEL

Imperial Hotel, Ha Yarkon Street 66,
Tel Aviv-Yafo

HOTEL
BAR

◆ TO VISIT BEFORE YOU DIE BECAUSE

You can taste goofy things in the small hours, especially if some local
bartenders from the neighbourhood have shown up.

Imperial Craft, with its trendy cocktails and Asian-inspired menu, turns cocktail shaking into a form of art. A favourite with local bartenders, who come here to relax after their shifts, this craft cocktail bar was also one of the first to open in Tel Aviv. The menu is subdivided into 'Fruity', 'Bitter', 'Smoked', 'Spirituous', 'Fresh', 'Exotic', 'Deep & Aged' and 'Spicy'. Clearly, there is something for everyone. The bar is decorated with elegance, which is echoed in the drinks in your glass.

— 134 —
WHISKEY
BAR & MUSEUM

ISRAEL

Tel Aviv
David Elazar Street 27, Sarona, Tel Aviv

COCKTAIL
BAR

◆ TO VISIT BEFORE YOU DIE BECAUSE

The bar stocks more than a thousand different whiskies from all over the world.

Whiskey Bar & Museum is where whisky lovers wish to go when they die. And also while still alive. This combination bar and whisky museum is located in the Templar tunnel in Sarona, which in the nineteenth century housed a winery and until a decade ago was used by Mossad. The bar stocks more than a thousand different whiskies from all over the world, from Scotland and Ireland to Hong Kong and India. All bottles on display in the museum can be tasted and purchased. Whiskies are served in 25-milliletre Glencairn Whiskey glasses, which bring out their taste and aroma beautifully.

— 135 —
BAR BENFIDDICH

Tokyo

JAPAN

9/F 1-13-7 Nishi-shinjuku,
Shinjukuward, Tokyo

COCKTAIL
BAR

◆ TO VISIT BEFORE YOU DIE BECAUSE
This is the place to enjoy the chartreuses from Tarragona.

Bartending starts at home for Hiroyasu Kayama. He transformed the nursery in his home just north of Tokyo into the drying room for the herbs that he grows. His own room is said to be where he stores his famous home-made absinthe. Expect the unexpected in this small ninth-floor bar. A tip: whatever he wants to do, let him, because he is sure to surprise you. Perhaps he will go for one of his unusual infusions or a vintage liqueur. Or maybe he will mix up a perfect cocktail. His drinks are enormously popular, so expect the place to be packed. If it is, then move on to Kayama's Bar B & F, located in the same building. This bar focuses on brandy and elixir. It is an easy stroll from one bar to the other, even when you have had one (or two) too many ...

— 136 —
BAR HIGH FIVE

JAPAN

Tokyo
Efflore Ginza 5 Bldg.
BF, 5-4-15 Ginza, Tokyo

**COCKTAIL
BAR**

◆ TO VISIT BEFORE YOU DIE BECAUSE

You will be served at the bar with unparalleled refinement and class.
Do not let the house rules posted on the wall scare you.
The staff only want what is best for their fans. Hats off!

Bar High Five is a classic bar with dreamy background music, hip guests and fantastic bartenders. Located in the trendy Ginza district, it is a modest space looking out over the Ginza railway tracks. Cocktail mixing and stirring has been raised to the category of art here: head bartender and owner Hidetsugo Ueno carefully mixes up creative drinks that will take your taste buds by surprise. Ask for a 'Bamboo' and you will soon know what we mean. The place is small, but the intimacy is part of its appeal. Do not bother looking for a cocktail menu, because there is none. Instead, the bartenders will ask about your preferences and then proceed to fix you a tailor-made cocktail. Bar High Five also boasts an impressive collection of well over 200 Japanese and Scotch whiskies. They do not take reservations, but if you insist they keep you a place at the bar, your seat will be reserved for only ten minutes. So ... run!

BAR/S

JAPAN

Tokyo
104-0061 Tokyo,
Chūō, Ginza, 8 Chome-8-3

COCKTAIL
BAR

◆ TO VISIT BEFORE YOU DIE BECAUSE

The bar has an amazing location on the 11th floor and you will be fascinated
by all the things you encounter on your way up.

BAR/S is a trendy cocktail bar within the
Shiseido building in Tokyo's Ginza district.
The bar is divided into two separate spaces:
a casual area and a fully equipped lounge.
Tasty, refined dishes are served alongside a
wide selection of cocktails, wine, champagne
and, of course, sake. It is the ideal rest stop
after a long day shopping in the district.

parlour.shiseido.co.jp/bar/s/

— 138 —
BAR TRAM

JAPAN

Tokyo
2/F, 1-7-13 Ebisunishi, Shibuya, Tokyo

COCKTAIL
BAR

TO VISIT BEFORE YOU DIE BECAUSE
The bar also serves exceptional cold-brew coffee.

Bar Tram is Bar Trench's big brother and lies only a few blocks away. This typical speakeasy bar also specialises in absinthe and whisky. Both Bar Trench and Bar Tram are managed by Takuya Ito, a real absinthe connoisseur. Just like at Bar Trench, absinthe is presented in the classical way, that is, poured on a sugar cube that is held over your glass with a specially designed absinthe spoon. Do you prefer your absinthe as part of a cocktail? Then ask for the 'Bitter End', which also contains Cointreau, lemon and orange.

— 139 —
BAR TRENCH

JAPAN

Tokyo
1-5-8 Ebisunishi, Shibuya, Tokyo

COCKTAIL
BAR

TO VISIT BEFORE YOU DIE BECAUSE
Talking to the manager/bartender with the Zorro moustache and the Portugese roots in Portuguese immediately breaks the ice. Another tip: ask for a cocktail based on Nikka whisky.

This magical cocktail bar (Bar Tram's little sister) lies hidden in the streets of Ebisu, near the train station. No doubt thanks to head bartender Rogerio Vaz's weakness for absinthe, Bar Trench stocks a wide range of herbal liqueurs that he will gladly tell you all about. The cocktails, too, are inspiring and lively. Do try the artichoke mojito, or the 'Go Lassi' with absinthe, lime, dill, cucumber and yogurt. While the drinks list is not extensive, it still does not make choosing any easier. The place has a Parisian vibe and the drinks are top-quality.

Strawberry Gin Fizz

Chill a tumbler glass.
Fill a shaker with ice cubes and the following:
→ 35 ml (7 teaspoons) Strawberry Gin Mombasa
→ 20 ml (4 teaspoons) strawberry puree
→ 10 ml (2 teaspoons) sugar syrup
→ 15 ml (1 tablespoon) lime juice

Shake hard for 25 seconds and serve in
the chilled glass. Garnish with a sprig of
mint and a fresh strawberry.

Cocktail
intermezzo

Twisted Rum Swizzle

Chill a tumbler glass.
Fill a shaker with ice cubes and the following:
→ 60 ml (1/4 cup) Dictador Rum Aged 12 Years
→ 5 ml (1 teaspoon) Falernum
→ 5 ml (1 teaspoon) Forest Maraschino liqueur
→ 30 ml (2 tablespoons) lime juice
→ 20 ml (4 teaspoons) sugar syrup

Shake hard, strain into the chilled glass and fill
up with crushed ice. Garnish to taste.

Gin Fizz

Chill a large tumbler glass.
Fill a shaker with ice cubes and the following:
→ 1 dash (0.625 ml or 1/8 teaspoon) egg white
→ 30 ml (2 tablespoons) soda
→ 60 ml (1/4 cup) The Botanist gin
→ 30 ml (2 tablespoons) lime juice
→ 20 ml (4 teaspoons) lime syrup

Shake hard and serve in the chilled glass.
Garnish with a slice of lime.

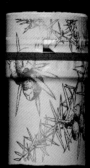

Cocktail
intermezzo

Vermouth Tonic

Fill a long-drink glass with ice cubes
and the following:
→ 50 ml (1/5 cup) Martini Riserva Ambrato
→ 15 ml (1 tablespoon)
   Erasmus Bond Tonic Classic

Garnish with the zest of a blood orange

Rob Roy

Chill a coupette glass.
Fill a shaker with ice cubes and the following:
→ 60 ml (1/4 cup) Taketsuru Non Age
  (Japanese whisky)
→ 20 ml (4 teaspoons) Forest Vermouth Red
→ 3 dashes (1.875 ml or 3/8 teaspoon)
  Angostura bitters

Shake and then strain into the coupette glass.
Garnish with a cherry (optional).

Sidecar

Chill a coupette glass.
Fill a shaker with ice cubes and the following:
→ 50 ml (1/5 cup) Cognac Pierre Ferrand 1840
→ 30 ml (2 tablespoons) lime juice
→ 15 ml (1 tablespoon) Cointreau Blood Orange
→ 15 ml (1 tablespoon) Cointreau Dark
→ 10 ml (2 teaspoons) orange cordial

Shake for 20 seconds and strain into
the chilled glass. Garnish with orange zest.

— 140 —
COBBLER BAR

AUSTRALIA

Brisbane
7 Browning Street,
West End, QLD 4101, Brisbane

COCKTAIL
BAR

◆ TO VISIT BEFORE YOU DIE BECAUSE

When you ask for an 'Old-Fashioned', the bartenders will let you choose from one of their 400 whiskies.

Cobbler is a cool whisky and cocktail lounge decorated like a loft. Once inside you will find a whole wall lined not with books, but with whisky and tequila. Cobbler pulls out all the stops to offer everyone a complete whisky experience. Its whisky menu is divided into 'Beginners', 'Tasting' and 'Masters' levels, and 'Barman's Friend'. But it is not only whisky and tequila lovers who will be in their respective heavens here; other guests, too, are sure to find something to their liking on the fabulous cocktail menu and its 'Tiki', 'Old-Fashioned', and 'Classic' categories. In the unlikely scenario that you have not found something to your palate's taste, bar owner Martin will fix you your very own perfect drink. No food is served here, but you are welcome to bring your own snacks or dishes from home or from the surrounding restaurants.

www.cobblerbar.com

SEYMOUR'S
COCKTAILS & OYSTERS

AUSTRALIA

Brisbane
19 Caxton Street,
Petrie Terrace, QLD 4000, Brisbane

**COCKTAIL
BAR**

◆ TO VISIT BEFORE YOU DIE BECAUSE

The bar is an ode to the New Orleans of the 1920s.

This bar takes you back to New Orleans in 1920 and in particular to the notorious red-light district of Storyville. The cocktails, too, pay homage to the city: think 'Sazerac', 'Hurricane', 'Julep', etc. Of course the bar plays jazz music and serves fresh oysters. This trendy cocktail bar is an initiative by the team behind Lefty's Old Time Music Hall, an equally cool bar featuring live music. Seymour's interior looks rather 'shady', but this is exactly one of the elements that gives it this typical feel of New Orleans at the turn of the twentieth century. Red carpet, vibrant wallpaper, mirrors and vintage posters set the tone.

— 142 —
ATRIUM BAR ON 35

AUSTRALIA

Melbourne
Sofitel Hotel, 25 Little Collins Street,
VIC 3000, Melbourne

HOTEL
BAR

◆ TO VISIT BEFORE YOU DIE BECAUSE

The interior's strong, flashy colours give the Atrium Bar a very luxurious air.
And that's without counting the menu's twenty champagnes that often vary
from one glass to another.

The Atrium Bar On 35 is a chic bar on the
35th floor of the Sofitel, from which the
view of the city is absolutely spectacular.
The bar's ambience is Christmas-like all
through the year. In other words, when you
enter this bar, you will start getting a warm,
fuzzy feeling inside, and even more so after
a couple of glasses of champagne.

— 143 —
THE EVERLEIGH

	Melbourne	
AUSTRALIA	150–156 Gertrude Street, Fitzroy, VIC 3065, Melbourne	COCKTAIL BAR

◆ TO VISIT BEFORE YOU DIE BECAUSE

The Everleigh lifts classic cocktails to new heights, and do try out the jazz evenings.

The Everleigh is every cocktail nerd's nirvana. Its skilled baristas will guide you through the extensive menu with a smile. The bar has won numerous awards, including spots on the highly competitive 'World's 50 Best Bars' list in 2013 and 2014.

Be sure to pick a place at the bar, because the bartenders' skills are a delight to behold. The 'Red Grasshopper' is a must-try. Its tequila, honey, lemon and smoked pepper will give you an instant kick.

www.theeverleigh.com

BLACK PEARL

Melbourne

AUSTRALIA

304 Brunswick Street,
Fitzroy, VIC 3065, Melbourne

COCKTAIL
BAR

◆ TO VISIT BEFORE YOU DIE BECAUSE

The Black Pearl stands out for its hospitality:
here you will feel pleased as Punch.

The Black Pearl has carried off quite a few awards. No fewer than four Bartender of the Year winners have shaken and stirred here. And yet this family business retains its modesty, preferring to focus on being a cosy place where locals can go to enjoy a perfectly served cocktail. Behind the bar you will find some of Melbourne's top hospitality experts. Their creativity and professionalism shine through in every drink. Whether it be a classic gin and tonic or a molecular cocktail, all are prepared with the utmost care. The Black Pearl also stands out for its warm reception: here you will feel in heaven. It is so relaxing you will want to stay on for a long, long time ...

1806

AUSTRALIA

Melbourne
169 Exhibition Street, VIC 3000,
Melbourne

COCKTAIL
BAR

◆ TO VISIT BEFORE YOU DIE BECAUSE

1806 guarantees lovely drinks and discretion.
No wonder so many celebrities come here.

1806 is a very special cocktail bar in Melbourne that was founded in 2007 and offers a wide assortment of classic cocktails. Its name refers to the year in which the word 'cocktail' is thought to have appeared for the first time. The bartenders' amazing attention to detail attracts droves of well-known mixologists from all over the world who come here to sample the drinks. The award-winning menu pays homage to the history of the cocktail by having one from almost every decade. The various drinks are guaranteed to please all palates and are accompanied by a short but informative anecdote about their origin. Every three months the cocktail menu is updated with seasonal products. Not in the mood for a cocktail? They have an impressive whisky list and also produce their own draught beer. Robert De Niro is a regular guest and a great fan of their martinis. The bar's manager and owner have even published a cocktail book. No doubt about it: 1806 has become a real Australian institution.

— 146 —
ABODE
BISTRO & BAR

AUSTRALIA

Sydney
150 Day Street, Sydney, NSW 2000

COCKTAIL
BAR

◆ TO VISIT BEFORE YOU DIE BECAUSE

**This is a sports bar, stylish bistro,
lounge bar and second home all rolled into one.**

This bistro and bar, near Sydney's Darling Harbour, stands out for its multifunctionality: a place that feels like home, but also a sports bar, a stylish bistro or a lounge bar in which to spend a night out with your friends. The 'shared-dining' concept adds an extra touch of homeliness.

Abode uses nothing but seasonal products, both in its food and in its drinks, of which the menu lists about 25. Be sure to try one of the dessert cocktails, like the 'Cookies & Cream', which is made with Baileys, vanilla syrup, cream and Crème de Cacao.

BAXTER INN

AUSTRALIA

Sydney
152–156 Clarence Street,
Sydney, NSW 2000

COCKTAIL
BAR

◆ TO VISIT BEFORE YOU DIE BECAUSE

They have an eye for detail, serving top-notch whiskies in brandy glasses.

Picture this. A rough-and-tough whisky bar down an abandoned alleyway with a few smokers standing next to the entrance. The Baxter Inn has a huge whisky collection that you will only reluctantly leave behind when you are forced out at closing time. Behind the bar are shelves upon shelves full of whisky bottles. The cocktails, ranging from classics to contemporary blends, will also make your jaw drop, but to be honest, what you come here for is the atmosphere and the whisky. The Baxter Inn is one of the coolest places in Sydney today. Make sure you try their home-made pretzels!

— 148 —
BETA BAR

AUSTRALIA

Sydney
238 Castlereagh Street,
Sydney, NSW 2000

**COCKTAIL
BAR**

◆ TO VISIT BEFORE YOU DIE BECAUSE

They serve delicious martinis in white-marble martini glasses.

Beta Bar is located above Alpha, a popular Sydney restaurant. It is an initiative by the Hellenic Club, an association founded by the Australian city's Greek community in 1924. Expect dramatic decoration, generous mezze dishes and cocktails with a hedonistic twist. Needless to say, they serve nice ouzo, and should you get hungry, you cannot go wrong with their home-made moussaka.

www.betabarsydney.com.au

— 149 —
360 BAR AND DINING

AUSTRALIA

Sydney

Sydney Westfield Centre, Pitt Street,
Sydney, NSW 2000

COCKTAIL
BAR

◆ TO VISIT BEFORE YOU DIE BECAUSE

The view over Sydney Harbour is so breathtaking you will almost forget to drink.

360 Bar and Dining offers visitors a breathtaking view of the city, and because it is a revolving restaurant, you will be able to see almost every corner of Sydney right from your table. You can start dinner with a kangaroo carpaccio while watching the sun go down, and finish with a duck confit while the lights of Sydney Harbour flicker distantly in the background. Do try out a seat at the bar, too: the ideal place for a date over an 'Old- Fashioned', with a glorious view.

AUSTRALIA	**Sydney** 2/40 King Street, Sydney, NSW 2000	COCKTAIL BAR

◆ TO VISIT BEFORE YOU DIE BECAUSE

What makes PS40 so exceptional is the fact that it makes its own sodas with local ingredients.

What makes PS40 so exceptional is its sodas, home-made with local ingredients. Pair these natural lemonades with one of its house spirits and you will have a first-class cocktail. While the cocktails have been designed to put the bar's sodas in the spotlight, you can also expect to find unusual ingredients in your glass, such as smoked miso caramel, spicy yoghurt, beer pretzel reductions, etc. Delicious sandwiches and trendy bar food are available too.

About the author

> Jurgen Lijcops is an excellent taster who not only has a near-encyclopedic knowledge of drinks but also is a naturally gifted host and entertainer.
> — Peter Goossens, Hof van Cleve

Jurgen Lijcops studied at the Burgundy Wine School in Beaune and then went to work as an assistant sommelier at the renowned Scholteshof restaurant. After becoming head sommelier at the Scholteshof, Lijcops moved to the two-star Slagmolen restaurant in Opglabbeek. Next, he was promoted to maître sommelier at the three-star Bruneau restaurant in Brussels. He subsequently worked as manager of the ambitious Withof project at the castle of Brasschaat. In 2009 he opened the Glorious on Antwerp's Zuid. It immediately became one of the city's leading restaurants, even gaining a Michelin star. In 2016 he set up Bar Burbure, which was proclaimed 'Best Bar Concept' that very same year. Lijcops has twice been named best sommelier in Belgium and best host in Belgium by Gault-Millau. Constantly striving to update his knowledge of drinks, he travels the world, discovering the most exquisite bars in which to sit back and sip the best cocktails and spirits.

About Bar Burbure

> Jurgen Lijcops is doing a great deal for the Belgian bar scene with Bar Burbure, establishing a high-end cocktail bar that can compete with those in London, Milan and New York! A must-visit when in Belgium!
> — Ran van Ongevalle, winner of the Global Bacardi Legacy competition

> True class and style with the finest spirit selection and clever cocktails! Very well done!
> — Martin Hudak, the Savoy's American Bar, London

> I had a wonderful time at Bar Burbure; the details of both the venue and the service make for a destination drinking experience, not only in Belgium but surely in Europe!
> — Remy Savage, head bartender, Artesian, London

Amid gorgeous green tiles and modern copper fixtures, patrons can enjoy the finest of cocktails in a cosy, well-appointed corner bar in Antwerp's museum district. With a full bar, including premium-label liquors, liqueurs, cognacs and whiskys, plus its own trademark Forest line of specialty spirits, **Bar Burbure** offers you an array of delicious libations. The carefully curated wine list changes seasonally. Beer aficionados will be delighted to discover the Westvleteren Trappist range, plus the renowned Czech-crafted Pilsner Urquell on tap. Bar Burbure has a fine selection of Spanish sherries from Bodegas Tradición, and cigars are available for enjoying outside on the terrace. See how fashionable Milan, quaint London and cosmopolitan Manhattan all blend together in Bar Burbure, making it Antwerp's epicentre for relaxing and unwinding in quiet sophistication.

Index

Photo credits

p. 8 Jeroen Hanselaer / p. 10 Thomas Hart Shelby / p. 11 Christian Seel / p. 12 Untitled Supper Club / p. 13 Courtesy of Bordel / p. 14 Imageselect / p. 15 Imageselect / p. 16 Courtesy of The Cosmopolitan of Las Vegas / p. 17 Courtesy of the Cosmopolitan of Las Vegas (Erik Kabik) / p. 18 Courtesy of Millennium Biltmore Los Angeles / p. 19 Benoit Linero / pp. 20 – 23 The Spare Room / pp. 24 -25 Adrian Boot & Island Outpost Images / p. 26 Jochen Hirschfeld / p. 27 Image provided by Hotel Monteleone / p. 28 – 29 BlackTail / p. 30 The Beekman, a Thompson Hotel / p. 31 The Blond at 11 Howard Hotel / pp. 32 – 33 Gerber Group / pp. 34 – 35 Dante New York City / pp. 36 – 37 Brent Herrig / pp. 38 – 39 Emilie Baltz / p. 40 Daniel Krieger / p. 41 Imageselect / p. 42 Scott Gordon Bleicher / p. 43 Addison Hospitality Group / p. 44 Noah Fecks / p. 45 Ines Leong / p. 46 Allison Webber / p. 47 W Santiago Hotel / p. 48 Canon Bar / p. 49 Megan Rainwater / pp. 50 – 51 AJ Fernando / pp. 52 – 57 Jurgen Lijcops / p. 58 Flying Dutchmen Cocktails / p. 59 Tales & Spirits / p. 60 (links) Frederik Picard (rechts) Bart D'hooge / p. 61 Nullam Microwaveum / pp. 62 – 63 Didier Van den Broeck / pp. 64 – 65 Hotel Grande Bretagne, a Luxury Collection Hotel / pp. 66 – 67 Kosmas Koumianos / p. 68 Eva Langue / p. 69 Imageselect / pp. 70 – 71 Javier de las Muelas / pp. 72 – 73 The Edgbaston / pp. 74 – 77 EquinoxLightPhoto / pp. 78 – 79 Volker Seibert / p. 80 Jack Hardy / p. 81 Imageselect / pp. 82 – 83 Zannier Hotels / pp. 84 – 85 Zaza Bertrand / p. 86 © 2017 Andy Davies & HR Giger Museum / p. 87 Stephan Lemke / pp. 88 – 89 Swetlana Holz / p. 90 Soho House Istanbul / p. 91 Kilimanjaro / pp. 92 – 93 Gra Z Vognem / p. 94 Stollen 1930, Kufstein / p. 95 Humberto Mouro & Jorge Simão / pp. 96 – 97 Nick Taylor / pp. 98 – 99 The Alchemist / p. 100 aqua shard / p. 101 – 103 Charlotte Faith / p. 104 Erik Lorincz / p. 105 Fairmont Hotels / p. 106 Connaught Bar / pp. 107 – 109 The Bloomsbury / p. 110 Christopher's Martini Bar / p. 111 German Gymnasium / pp. 112 – 113 Artesian / p. 114 – 115 Tom Elms / p. 116 Paul Winch – Furness / p. 117 Marriott Hotels / p. 118 K Bar / p. 119 – 121 Jarek Klocinski / pp. 122 – 123 Johnny Stephens / p. 124 Mr Fogg's / p. 125 Jerome Courtial / pp. 126 – 129 Jerome Courtial / pp. 130 – 131 Lloyd Sturdy / pp. 132 – 133 Aqua Restaurant Group / p. 134 69 Colebrook Row / p. 135 Sky Pod Bar / p. 136 Park Chinois / pp. 137 – 139 The Zetter Town House Clerkenwell / p. 140 Le Parfum / p. 141 City Space Bar & Restaurant / p. 142 Schumann's GmbH / pp. 143 – 145 Alescha Birkenholz / p. 146 Allison Webber / p. 147 Castor Club / pp. 148 – 149 Roberta Valerio / p. 150 Dirty Dick / p. 151 Four Seasons Paris / p. 152 Prangé / p. 153 Eric Laignel / p. 154 (above) Philippe Levy (below) Sherry Butt / p. 155 Hemingway Bar / pp. 156 – 157 The Jerry Thomas Project / pp. 158 – 159 Nicke Jacobsson / p. 160 Mr Simon Bar / p. 161 Harry's Bar / pp. 162 – 163 Café Bar Baiser / pp. 164 – 169 Jurgen Lijcops / p. 170 Widder Hotel / p. 171 Lebua Hotel / pp. 172 – 173 Mandarin Oriental, Bangkok / p. 174 Centara Hotels & Resorts / pp. 175 – 177 Anantara Sathorn Bangkok Hotel / p. 178 Gold on 27 / p. 179 Vault bar, JW Marriott Marquis Dubai / p. 180 Mandarin Oriental, Hong Kong / pp. 181 – 183 Millimeter Interior Design Limited / p. 184 Club Qing / p. 185 Djapa Bar / p. 186 Dr Fern's Gin Parlour / pp. 187 – 189 Michael Perini and Sunny Hung / p. 190 Lobster Bar and Grill at Island Shangri-La, Hong Kong / p. 191 Shangri-La Hotel Hong Kong / p. 192 Michael Perini/ p. 193 Otto e Mezzo Bombana / p. 194 The Landmark Mandarin Oriental, Hong Kong / p. 195 Quinary / pp. 196 – 197 Stockton / pp. 198 – 199 Henry Wilson / p. 200 Ayana Resort & Spa / p. 201 Four Seasons Hotel Mumbai / pp. 202 – 203 Four Seasons Hotel Seoul, photography: Ken Seet / p. 204 Speak Low / p. 205 Imageselect / pp. 206 – 209 EK Yap and Atlas Bar / p. 210 Employees Only Singapore / p. 211 Tippling Club / pp. 212 – 213 Tawan C. Photography / p. 214 Tawan C. Photography / p. 215 Raffles Singapore / pp. 216 – 217 Manhattan at Regent Singapore, A Four Seasons Hotel / p. 218 Jana Ensof / p. 219 Smoke & Mirrors / p. 220 Ben Yuster / pp. 221 – 223 Cookoo Studio / p. 224 Bar Benfiddich / p. 225 High Five / p. 226 Imageselect / p. 227 Bar Tram / pp. 228 – 229 Bar Trench / pp. 230 – 235 Jurgen Lijcops / pp. 236 – 237 Cobbler Bar / p. 238 Seymour's Cocktails & Oysters / p. 239 Sofitel, photographers: Shellie Froidevaux & Karen Woo / p. 240 James Morgan / p. 241 Ryan Noreiks / pp. 242 – 243 Jack Hawkins / p. 244 Abode Bistro & Bar / p. 245 Baxter Inn / pp. 246 – 247 Beta Bar Sydney / p. 248 360 Bar and Dining / p. 249 – 251 Alana Dimou / p. 253 Jeroen Hanselaer

Colophon

Texts
Jurgen Lijcops
Isabel Boons

Translation
Xavier De Jonge

Copy-editing
Linda Schofield

Back Cover Image:
EK Yap & Atlas Bar, Singapore

Book Design
ASB

This book is
MARKED

MARKED is an initiative
by Lannoo Publishers
www.marked-books.com

Sign up for our MARKED newsletter with news
about new and forthcoming publications on art,
interior design, food & travel, photography and
fashion as well as exclusive offers and events.

If you have any questions or comments about
the material in this book, please do not hesitate
to contact our editorial team: markedteam@
lannoo.com

© Lannoo Publishers, Belgium, 2018
D/2018/45/22 – NUR 450 / 500
ISBN: 9789401449120
3rd print run 2019
www.lannoo.com

#AREYOUMARKED